"Caryn Rivadeneira's *Known and [* ... found, funny, and affirming reflectic ... who are—to use her words—in the "heart-broadening season ... raising children. On days that can feel like they are never going to end, or at moments when we doubt that we are up to the task of mothering, this book will restore weary hearts. Rivadeneira reminds us of who we are to our Creator, and that, like the psalmists, we can always bring our whole, authentic selves to God. Highly recommend!"

—**Jennifer Grant**, author of *MOMumental* and *Love You More*

"*Known and Loved* offers moms a refreshing dip into the Psalms, bathing their souls with comfort and encouragement found in both honest lament *and* joyful praise. If you've ever wondered if God understands what you're going through, if he loves you when you make mistakes, if what you're doing *matters*—you need this book!"

—**Keri Wyatt Kent**, author of ten books, including *Deeply Loved*

"Although it seems counterintuitive that being surrounded by our children on a daily and hourly basis would result in feeling isolated and lonely, so often we feel exactly this way. We get caught up in the challenges of serving the seemingly endless needs and wants of our children and forget that we have minds, hearts, and souls that need to be nurtured as much as our kids do. But Caryn Rivadeneira's wonderful devotional reminds us that we *do* need to be cared for, and that our heavenly Father is longing to be the one to do so. Caryn's wise, witty, and warm words will help you enter into God's presence in a deeply reassuring and comforting way as you experience anew his desire to know and love you and discover that you are far from alone in your journey of motherhood."

—**Helen Lee**, author of *The Missional Mom*

Known
and
Loved

52 DEVOTIONS FROM THE PSALMS

Caryn Rivadeneira

Revell

a division of Baker Publishing Group
Grand Rapids, Michigan

© 2013 by Caryn Rivadeneira

Published by Revell
a division of Baker Publishing Group
P.O. Box 6287, Grand Rapids, MI 49516-6287
www.revellbooks.com

Printed in the United States of America

Library of Congress Cataloging-in-Publication Data is on file at the Library of Congress, Washington, DC.

ISBN 978-0-8007-2207-4 (pbk.)

Scripture quotations are from the Holy Bible, New International Version®. NIV®. Copyright © 1973, 1978, 1984, 2011 by Biblica, Inc.™ Used by permission of Zondervan. All rights reserved worldwide. www.zondervan.com

The internet addresses, email addresses, and phone numbers in this book are accurate at the time of publication. They are provided as a resource. Baker Publishing Group does not endorse them or vouch for their content or permanence.

The author is represented by Alive Communications, Inc.

13 14 15 16 17 18 19   7 6 5 4 3 2 1

To Henrik, Greta, and Fredrik
How wonderful it is to know and love you!

Contents

Acknowledgments

While authors are alone when we write, no book happens without the help of others—and that help takes many different shapes.

So, first off, thank you to all the moms in my life who have shared the stories and bits of truth that helped shape this devotional.

To my own mom, Catherine Dahlstrand, who encouraged me through this writing process and encourages me in mothering.

To the moms in my family, friend, and neighbor circles who've shared stories of how God has worked through motherhood (mostly without ever thinking they'd end up in a book! But I'm a writer; they should know better, right?). And to all the moms I've met at MOPS and other mom groups around the country. So many courageous and wonderful moms are doing great things in this world! It's exciting to see what God is up to through you all.

Thanks to my agent, Andrea Heinecke, who introduced me to this project and got the whole shebang rolling, and to Jean Blackmer, whose early guidance helped shape the idea.

Thanks to Rev. Tracey Bianchi, who listened to my first scattered thoughts about this project, saw sense through the mess, and gave good direction. And thanks to Carla Foote and Andrea Doering for becoming champions of the project.

Thanks, of course, to my amazing writer pals. Can't even imagine this writing life without all of you.

Special thanks to Rev. Gregg DeMey for acting as my Psalms expert and for not relinquishing that role even when I openly challenged his theological training (even though I have none) and questioned his Hebrew (when all I know is *shalom*). Shalom.

Thank you to the psalm writers themselves (hoping they can read this in heaven). Especially David. King David, what can I say? Thank you for sharing your heart, your mind, and your soul in such a beautiful and transparent way.

And, as always, thank you to my family: my husband, Rafi, my kids, Henrik, Greta, and Fredrik. Thank you for your "willingness" to let your life seep into my work and for putting up with my less-than-great moods as deadlines approach. You are all the best stories I've got going. And every time I see you I'm reminded that God's goodness and mercy surely *are* following me all the days of my life.

Introduction

Just Like David

What We Can Learn about Ourselves from Reading through the Psalms

After an hour of getting snacks, setting up toys, breaking up fights, setting time-out timers, wiping tears, forcing apologies, and putting kids back in time-outs, I had had enough. I needed to escape. To go into mama hiding.

So I settled the kids down, picked out a movie for them, grabbed a book for me, and snuck into my bedroom.

I eased the door closed behind me, straightened the comforter, set up the pillows, and double-slapped the mattress, inviting my dog to jump up and join me. *Alone at last. Just my book, my dog, and me.*

But then my Bible, there on my nightstand, caught my eye, and guilt zapped my heart. It had been a while since I last cracked open that Bible—at least by myself. Even my devotional life was now shared with my children. Nothing alone. Not even time with God.

With a dramatic sigh (to let God know what I was giving up for him!), I set down my novel and grabbed the Bible. It flipped open at its bookmark. To Psalm 1.

As good a place as any, I thought. And I began to read rather quickly through the familiar first psalm and the seemingly unrelatable second.

But then I stopped. My jaw dropped as I read tiny words—there just below Psalm 3—that would change the way I read the psalms, the way I would understand their writers. "A psalm of David," it said. And then, "When he fled from his son Absalom."

While the sadness of these simple lines' meaning sunk into my heart—David *fled* because his son wanted to kill him—another odd thought seeped into my brain. As I looked straight ahead at my closed door, listened to the murmur coming from my kids' movie on the other side of the wall, I realized that I had fled—in a way.

I'm just like David, I thought. But I immediately corrected myself.

Of course, I'm nothing like David. *He* had gone into hiding because Absalom wanted to *kill* him, to take over his throne. Although my kids were seemingly mutinous that day, really, they didn't want my duties.

David was an ancient, Middle-Eastern king. I am a modern, Midwestern mom.

David shepherded sheep, killed a giant, wrote lyrics, led armies, had housefuls of wives and concubines. I've *pet* sheep, killed giant *ants*, written blog posts, led armies of, well, nothing, and found one husband to be plenty, thank you very much.

And yet I *am* so much like David. I'm scared, but I'm arrogant. I'm desperate, but I'm thankful. I'm strong, but I'm humbled. I'm a misfit, but I'm uniquely gifted. I'm unlikely, but I'm called. I'm a sinner, but I'm forgiven. I'm a mess, but I'm beloved by God.

Most of the time I feel like a giant mix of a bunch of weird things, but I'm also fearfully and wonderfully made.

Just like David. Just like you.

While Psalms had long been a favorite book of mine, after that afternoon I dug back into it with renewed interest.

That day I went into hiding fell during a spell in my life when I felt lost as a mom and as a woman. My identity—both the way I saw myself and the way others saw me—somehow had gotten lost among the clutter down deep in the bottom of a toy bin. I wondered who I was—how and why God made me. I wondered what on earth my role in this world of his was.

As I began to revisit Psalms, I realized this book offers a gift beyond the sheer beauty of the lines and lyrics. In the psalms we peer directly into the writers' hearts, minds, and souls. We get raw and real with the authors (my "twin" David only wrote about half of them). We see them stumble; we see them succeed. We see them praise God; we see them wondering where God was. We see them assured; we see them confused.

The psalms let us see these people—people so different from and yet so like us—in their full, broken, and wonderful humanity. And in their quest to understand what that means, we see them seeking to understand God—and their roles in his world.

And because the psalms are the Word of God, we not only get to read the questions and longings of the people who wrote them, but we also get to hear God speak to *us* about how he made us, how he sees us, how he loves us. In the psalms, *God* tells us who we are.

Once I understood that, reading through the psalms helped me begin to understand more about me, about who God created me to be, about my role, about who God says I am.

Perhaps most important, in this quest to find out more about *me*, I found out more about God—the God who loves each of us so much that he made us unique and wonderful and full of purpose. That purpose includes motherhood yet reaches far beyond it.

The God who loves us, hears us, forgives us. The God who is worthy of all our praise.

Whether you've read through the Bible many times, never picked it up before, or anywhere in between, you'll find that spending time in the psalms always nourishes us, feeds us. Sometimes in clear-cut, obvious ways, sometimes through the totally unexpected. Especially since these words were written three thousand years ago by people whose lives looked little like our own. And yet, the aches, the longings, the questions, and the worship—all of the human experience—remain the same. Remarkable, really.

So in the fifty-two devotions of this book—broken up into broad categories and individual themes about who *God* says you are—you'll encounter ancient text mingled with modern stories. But these quests to discover who we are and why God made us are timeless, universal. Even as we often feel so alone in our struggles.

Because we moms don't get enough alone time, I do hope you'll carve out some space to take some time with these devotions on your own. And I hope that you'll consider a separate, complete reading of Psalms. But I hope you'll take time to read through these devotions—either alone, with friends, or a combination of both—and spend time thinking, writing, drawing, or talking about just why God made you, how he gifted you, and why you're so wonderful to and loved by him.

PART 1

You Are Wonderfully Made

You have searched me, LORD,
    and you know me.
You know when I sit and when I rise;
    you perceive my thoughts from afar.
You discern my going out and my lying down;
    you are familiar with all my ways.
Before a word is on my tongue
    you, LORD, know it completely.
You hem me in behind and before,
    and you lay your hand upon me.
Such knowledge is too wonderful for me,
    too lofty for me to attain.

Where can I go from your Spirit?
    Where can I flee from your presence?
If I go up to the heavens, you are there;
    if I make my bed in the depths, you are there.
If I rise on the wings of the dawn,
    if I settle on the far side of the sea,
even there your hand will guide me,
    your right hand will hold me fast.
If I say, "Surely the darkness will hide me
    and the light become night around me,"

even the darkness will not be dark to you;
   the night will shine like the day,
   for darkness is as light to you.

For you created my inmost being;
   you knit me together in my mother's womb.
I praise you because I am fearfully and wonderfully made;
   your works are wonderful,
   I know that full well.
My frame was not hidden from you
   when I was made in the secret place,
   when I was woven together in the depths of the earth.
Your eyes saw my unformed body;
   all the days ordained for me were written in your book
   before one of them came to be.
How precious to me are your thoughts, God!
   How vast is the sum of them!
Were I to count them,
   they would outnumber the grains of sand—
   when I awake, I am still with you.

If only you, God, would slay the wicked!
   Away from me, you who are bloodthirsty!
They speak of you with evil intent;
   your adversaries misuse your name.
Do I not hate those who hate you, Lord,
   and abhor those who are in rebellion against you?
I have nothing but hatred for them;
   I count them my enemies.
Search me, God, and know my heart;
   test me and know my anxious thoughts.
See if there is any offensive way in me,
   and lead me in the way everlasting.

                                    Psalm 139

You Are Made Just Right

Psalm 139:13–14

For you created my inmost being;
  you knit me together in my mother's womb.
I praise you because I am fearfully and wonderfully made;
  your works are wonderful,
I know that full well.

I grew up skinny. One of those girls other kids mock for having "chicken legs." Adults felt free to scrunch up their faces, shake their heads, and "marvel" at how skinny I was, asking my mom if she ever fed me. More than one person wrapped their fingers around my wrist and declared how they could just "snap" me.

None of this was considered bullying at the time because, of course, even back in the 1970s and 1980s of my childhood—long before every model's and actress's collarbone jutted out under spaghetti straps—thin was in. So making fun of me, pretending to snap my arms, was a compliment, I suppose.

Of course, I didn't see it that way. It hurt. Made me feel like I had been made wrong.

Until one day—when I was probably ten—I read a magazine article that claimed that no matter how much butter you spread on their toast or whole milk you poured on their cereal, most naturally "skinny" kids probably wouldn't gain weight. It was a metabolism thing. "Just the way they are made," I remember reading.

When my mom—who had been following my pediatrician's suggestion to add more milkshakes and butter to my diet—read the article, she said, "Just what I thought. You're made just right."

I can't imagine better words a mom could say to her child. In that moment, my mom gave me assurance that no matter what anyone else said or thought about my skinniness or my snap-ability, I was made right.

Of course, this echoes exactly what God says about us in Psalm 139. The verse says God *knit* us together. Knitting is an intricate process. Requiring a plan and intention. Each stitch is done on purpose. With a goal in mind.

It says he, God, made us *fearfully* and *wonderfully*. The words in this verse in Hebrew mean that God made us with "heartfelt interest" and "uniquely." How great is that?

That means my being skinny was no mistake. And somehow useful. Same goes with every other "odd" bit I've ever felt about myself. While I may not be perfect (and I have plenty of areas to grow in), the way God made me—the body he gave me, the talents I have, my personality, my interests—are all intended. Not mistakes. No matter what anyone else says.

I'm made just the way I need to be. So are you. It's all part of his plan. You and I were made just right.

Response

God, thank you for creating me. Thank you for taking your time, for thinking me through, for imagining who I'd be and what I'd do with the gifts you knit right into me. I'm humbled and amazed that I get to be your very own handiwork and that you made me to do great things.

What does God say? See Ephesians 2:10.

You Are Gifted

Psalm 57:7–8

My heart, O God, is steadfast,
    my heart is steadfast;
    I will sing and make music.
Awake, my soul!
    Awake, harp and lyre!
    I will awaken the dawn.

I get up early. And no longer just because I have to. It's no longer because a baby is crying or fussing, no longer because my preschooler is pulling at my covers, eager for some cartoons and cereal, no longer because the dog needs to be let out.

I get up early for something I never thought I'd be able to do: enjoy "quiet time." So at 5:30 every morning, I get up, grab my Bible and my laptop out of my office, put on the coffee, and wrap myself up in an afghan on the living room sofa. I crack open my Bible (right now I'm reading through Acts). I read a few verses, then close my eyes, letting the words trickle down through my mind, into my heart, then linger in my soul. Then I pray—lately, it's been the Lord's Prayer.

By then, the coffeepot has beeped ready, and so after unwrapping myself and getting a cup, I push my Bible over and open my laptop, checking email and Facebook before opening up a file, whichever project needs working on.

While to some it might seem that with the opening of the laptop my worship time has ended, it feels the opposite to me. My time of Bible reading, quiet reflection, and prayer is sweet. No question about that. But so is my "quiet time" of writing, of working.

Some days I "feel" very little when I read the Word of God; nothing jumps off the page, the words *do* nothing as they trickle through my self. While some days praying the Lord's Prayer (or any prayer) brings me into such tight communion with God—feeling like a tunnel runs straight between me and God—other days, it's like I'm talking to myself.

But when I write, when the words flow and the ideas come (or even when they don't and I'm just writing for writing's sake), I always feel God's presence. When I write, it becomes worship. I know he is near.

In the movie *Chariots of Fire*, Eric Liddell—the Christian Olympic runner who refuses to race on the Sabbath—says, "God made me fast. And when I run, I feel his pleasure."

Whether Liddell actually said these words or whether they are the screenwriter's words doesn't matter. Either way, they speak truth.

God created each of us with gifts and abilities and talents—and God gave them to be used. Just as it gives you pleasure to watch your child enjoy and play with a toy or gift you have given them, so does God enjoy watching us use our gifts. No matter what they are.

I love that in this passage David wakes up ready to make music (certainly one of David's gifts). I love that it's the way he "awakens the dawn," ushers in the day. I love that he uses the talents God gave him to thank God, to praise him.

Because he knows God smiles when we make use of what we've been given. Using our gifts—whether as a writer, a runner, a baker, a lawyer, a homemaker, a mother, an accountant, a gardener, a teacher, a whatever—is a form of worship and thanksgiving.

Let's not miss out on the opportunity to worship and feel God's pleasure as we use our gifts.

Response

God, you created me with gifts that were meant to be used— not buried. I will use these gifts, share these talents with the world, in the best way I can. It glorifies you when I do.

What does God say? See Romans 12.

You Are Known

Psalm 139:1–3

> You have searched me, LORD,
>   and you know me.
> You know when I sit and when I rise;
>   you perceive my thoughts from afar.
> You discern my going out and my lying down;
>   you are familiar with all my ways.

Moms tend to be a dismissed bunch. I mean, how often have you told someone you were a mom and they responded by saying, "Really? Fascinating! Tell me more about that." I'm going to go ahead and guess never.

When people hear that we are moms, they start asking about our kids. And because we love our kids, we gladly start talking about them. This may seem all well and good for a while, but it can lead to some devastating consequences.

I've spent good chunks of time as a mom feeling like not only did no one *really* know me, but also that I wasn't really worth knowing.

But this just isn't true. God knows us. And he thinks we are worth knowing.

Consider these words from the famous Psalm 139: "You know when I sit and when I rise. . . . You discern my going out and my lying down." God knows this about us! He knows when we sit (ahem: never). He knows when we rise (ahem: about four hundred times a night). He knows when we go out (ahem: not enough). And when we lie down (ahem: or crash into bed).

But seriously, how many people's sitting and lying-down habits do you know? I can tell you when my husband and my kids sit and lie down. If my parents and brother keep the same schedule they did when I was a kid, I can guess. These are intimate, personal details to know about someone. Things you only pay attention to if you are really, really interested and really, really crazy about the person.

This is how God feels about us.

We are worth knowing. And we are known. By God. How amazing is that?

So while the world may not always find us moms fascinating, God does. While others may not always know what our crazy or boring or somewhere-in-between days look like, God does. And while not everyone may know our deepest longings, the things we miss about our "old" lives, our hopes and dreams, our worries, our frustrations, our failures, and our victories, God does. With all the excitement and thrills and interesting things happening across the universe, God finds us fascinating.

Response

God, thank you for noticing when I get up at night, when I'm desperate for rest and a chance to sit. Thank you for noticing when I struggle to grab just a few moments alone. What a comfort it is to know that even when no one else seems to notice me or what I do, God on high searches me and knows me.

What does God say? See Psalm 139.

You Are Given Unique Desires

Psalm 37:4

Take delight in the LORD,
and he will give you the desires of your heart.

I know I'm not the only person who read Psalm 37:4 and finally wondered if it was less about God giving me whatever my heart *desired* and more about placing desires in my heart. But it doesn't matter, because the discovery was profound in my life. Especially as a mom who wondered if my desires could ever actually be fulfilled while busying about life with three young kids.

I'm pretty sure we've all been there, had those times when our hearts could explode with longing to live out our gifts, to just for one day indulge in something we care deeply about that might have little to do with our kids. I'm pretty sure that most of us have felt that we had dreams and desires left unfilled in life and were doubtful that they'd ever be lived out.

That's why my reading of this verse anew was so powerful to me. The day I read it, I had been in that place, convinced that my life desires were worthless, a mistake. I couldn't imagine being able to do the things I longed to do. I was ready to toss those dreams and desires in the trash.

Until I read this verse and, I believe, the Holy Spirit infused this other meaning for me—for all of us who are so buried under more urgent demands of life (read: kids!) that we start to believe that God made a mistake with us.

When we believe God himself places our desires in our hearts, it changes everything. Remember as well the simple but true words we tell others: "God doesn't make mistakes." This verse is such encouragement to moms who feel lost and trapped and undervalued and for those of us who feel we need to give up all our silly dreams and desires.

Not so. If—this verse says—we delight ourselves in the Lord, if we follow him, seek him, choose him, he's the one calling us forward with those desires. And God doesn't make mistakes. He'll provide a way and a time for those desires to turn into reality.

Response

God, thank you for inviting me into your presence, welcoming me to turn to you with my dreams and desires. Please show me how to use these desires of my heart in this world for your glory.

What does God say? See Matthew 7:7–8.

PART 2

You Are Held by God

A psalm of David. When he fled from his son Absalom.

Lord, how many are my foes!
> How many rise up against me!
Many are saying of me,
> "God will not deliver him."

But you, Lord, are a shield around me,
> my glory, the One who lifts my head high.
I call out to the Lord,
> and he answers me from his holy mountain.

I lie down and sleep;
> I wake again, because the Lord sustains me.
I will not fear though tens of thousands
> assail me on every side.

Arise, Lord!
> Deliver me, my God!
Strike all my enemies on the jaw;
> break the teeth of the wicked.

From the Lord comes deliverance.
> May your blessing be on your people.

Psalm 3

You Are Held by God

Psalm 34:18

> The LORD is close to the brokenhearted
> and saves those who are crushed in spirit.

I first underlined the simple and lovely words of Psalm 34:18 during the summer after my sophomore year of high school. That summer was one of the best ever. I turned sixteen, got my license, even got a car! But the summer was not without its trials—of the teenage angst variety. It was, after all, the summer I discovered heartache. Or, more specifically, heart*break*. It was the first—but not last— time that I'd liked a boy who, unfortunately, liked my friend.

While many of my memories of that heartbroken, sixteen-year-old me seem a bit silly and certainly overly dramatic to me today, when my mind returns to that image of me, reading this passage on my bed with my legs crossed underneath my Bible, reaching for my pen on the nightstand, there's nothing silly about it. After all, in that reading of Psalm 34, I had discovered something astonishing. There is nothing silly about the wonder of discovering that God cares about our broken hearts, about our crushed spirits. That he cares about the hurts we may be too embarrassed to tell others about, that we may feel ashamed of. And there's definitely nothing silly about realizing that God not only *cares* about broken hearts, but that he stays close to us in our brokenness. And that he not only cares that our spirits are getting crushed, but that he sets out to save us.

No, there's nothing silly about realizing what this verse ultimately tells us: that God is a God who sees our hearts the moment they break, that he sees our spirits struggling under the weights of this life, and that in those moments, in those times, God holds us tight, together.

My life has included more heartbreak and more spirit-crushing circumstances than I wish it had. Because of that, I've returned to this passage, reread its words, more times than I can count. It sat with me, comforted me during infertility, at funerals, as relationships soured, as finances tanked. Never once during all my readings of those words have I failed to be amazed at what God does for us in those times.

As moms, heartbreak and spirit-weariness kind of go with the territory; sooner or later, our kids or circumstances involving them *will* break our hearts, will crush our spirits. It's never easy to go through trials that leave us feeling heartbroken or crushed, but because we know that God is close to us—*saving* us!—in those moments, they can be wonderful.

Response

My heart is broken, God, over many things. So I bring it to you as an offering and ask that even as you work to heal its breaks, you use it to help me see the brokenhearted all around me.

What does God say? See Psalm 51.

You Are Supported

Psalm 94:18–19

When I said, "My foot is slipping,"
  your unfailing love, LORD, supported me.
When anxiety was great within me,
  your consolation brought me joy.

I hadn't talked to my friend Jeanie much since she'd had her third baby a couple of months before. We'd had short snippets of conversation, but no real talks. With each of us having three young kids, that was a luxury neither of us could often afford. So seeing the caller ID announcing "Jeanie" and hearing her say that the kids were sleeping was great news. With my own kids settled into after-school activities, we could maybe catch up.

After small talk, the conversation quickly turned to the complexities of managing three kids. I told her how one friend told me that once you had three, any other additions were a cakewalk. It was three that somehow turned family into chaos.

Jeanie—one of six kids herself—said her mother would probably agree with this. But I could hear the anxiety in her voice—over all those hundreds of miles of airwaves. She talked of how much she weighed decisions about leaving the house. It just took so long, was so much work. Especially now that the weather had turned cold. Jeanie talked about her prayers for patience. How some days it was all she could do to hold on.

I knew exactly what she meant. Life with two tiny kids and a newborn made me feel like my feet were always slipping, as the psalmist writes. Like I never really had a grip on anything. My anxiety levels ran pretty high. I could sense the same was true for Jeanie.

When I read the words of Psalm 94:18–19, I imagine the psalmist walking along the edge of a cliff, a curving mountain road. Perhaps he's carrying something: weapons or a staff or lunch wrapped in cloth. I picture his foot occasionally skidding off the side, kicking pebbles down into the abyss. And I see myself there, in this place where there is so much to fear. While technically I am safe on that path, one false step could send me careening off, just like those pebbles.

Motherhood feels like that so often. For the moment, we are fine. Our kids are fine. We still have our sanity. But—wow—some days, it feels that we are getting ever closer to that edge, to slipping right off, does it not? That's where the anxiety comes from.

But this verse tells us God is in that picture, and the Lord's "unfailing love" supports us. So even though we may have to walk some harrowing roads as moms and as women, even though the cliff to our right seems pretty steep, God's love is steeper and deeper still and is what actually surrounds us and supports us. There is nowhere in this life or in this world where we can or will fall in which God—and his great love—will not be ready to catch us.

Response

God, some days I feel like the roaring fires and rushing waters of life are too much for me. And then I sense something that changes it all: You are with me. Thank you for not leaving my side. Please continue to let me know you are near, and please keep me from being afraid as I navigate difficult spots in life.

What does God say? See Isaiah 43.

You Are Sustained

Psalm 3:5

I lie down and sleep;
I wake again, because the LORD sustains me.

I wish when I thought of motherhood a different word popped into my head. A word like *loved* or *fulfilled* or *blessed*. But you know what comes to mind when I think about my life as a mother? *Tired.* Maybe even *exhausted.*

Then once we get that out of the way—only then—do I go back to thinking about all the wonderful things about being a mom.

But the tired bit is just too integral, too intertwined with my experience of motherhood. Still. Even though it's been a decade since my first sleepless nights as a new mom. Even though my youngest has been sleeping through the night for some time. I still find myself so worn out when I finally get into bed at night—when the kids are finally asleep, the kitchen at least mildly tidied, my work semi-caught-up-with—that I wonder if I'll wake up again. Not because I'll *die*, mind you, but just because I imagine I could sleep forever and still not be caught up on the rest I need as a mom.

And yet—somehow—every seven or eight hours after my head hits the pillow, the alarm on my phone buzzes. I reach over to snooze it. Ten minutes later, it buzzes again. This time, I "dismiss" it, swing my legs over the side of the bed, and stretch. Amazed I have the energy to get up, to face the day and all the exhausting and wonderful elements it entails.

And yet I'm grateful for this energy. I remember all too clearly the nights I'd be up several times—nursing, nursing, changing, nursing. I remember when I didn't need an alarm, when my babies let me know when I had to get up.

While my mornings—and my nights—are different (read: they are better!) now that my kids are no longer babies and my nights are no longer sleepless, a truth remains: motherhood exhausts me.

But God sustains me. He sustains you. That's what I love about Psalm 3:5. David wrote this while he was fleeing from his own son; his fears were of the life-and-death sort. Waking up meant he survived another night. Because God sustained him.

While we may not fear for our lives, this verse speaks to us—when we're so desperately tired, when we think we cannot possibly ever catch up on rest, when we feel we are too tired to face another day, when our exhaustion threatens to erase our sense of self, of purpose, God *sustains* us.

Merriam-Webster's online dictionary offers these as the first six definitions of *to sustain*: 1. To give support or relief to; 2. To supply with sustenance; nourish; 3. Keep up; prolong; 4. To support the weight of; prop; also: to carry or withstand; 5. To buoy up; and 6. To bear up under.

Imagine God doing this for you—in your most tired, most worn-out, most beat-down moments. Imagine God supporting and relieving you. Nourishing you. Keeping you. Carrying you. Buoying you. Imagine God bearing up under you.

Even in our most tired times, we rise again, held by, sustained by, buoyed by God.

Response

God, I am so tired, so worn out. Some days I'm convinced I won't have the energy to keep going. Please be my strength, Lord. Sustain me to do what I need to do.

What does God say? See Habakkuk 3.

You Are Heard

Psalm 6:6–9

I am worn out from my groaning.
All night long I flood my bed with weeping
and drench my couch with tears.
My eyes grow weak with sorrow;
they fail because of all my foes.
Away from me, all you who do evil,
for the LORD has heard my weeping.
The LORD has heard my cry for mercy;
the LORD accepts my prayer.

I've come to believe that to be a mom is to get used to not being heard. Whether it's calling the family to the table or asking a question while a child is watching cartoons, moms can get pretty used to being ignored, to wondering if they're really saying anything at all. I know that most of the times I've raised my voice to my kids, it's been out of frustration from *not being heard.*

And that not-being-heard feeling extends beyond the walls of our home. My fellow moms and I have talked more times than I can count about how it seems that once we became moms, part of the "identity crisis" we faced was the feeling that no one really heard—or cared about—what we had to say. Unless it's about our preferred brand of peanut butter or laundry detergent, often it seems that not many people are that interested in hearing what moms have to say.

This is a terrible feeling, this not being heard. It leaves us wondering if we're even worthy of being heard, if what we have to say really does matter.

My friend Mary became convinced that her voice did not matter, that within the cacophony of family life and the bigger voices out in the world, hers would always be drowned out. And no one would miss it. Mary figured as long as she was around to make breakfast, lunch, and dinner, available to hug her kids when they cried, to tidy up the house, and to take her turn working in the church nursery, that anything she had to *say* didn't really matter.

When her doctor diagnosed her with clinical depression and directed her to start seeing a therapist, this "voicelessness" was the first thing Mary told her therapist about. Not being heard has harsh consequences.

But here's the stunning reality: although our kids might ignore us and although the world may not always hear us as we long to be heard, *God* hears us. God on high hears our every word. And whether God is hearing our groaning and crying for help, as the psalmist writes, or whether he is hearing us ramble on about our days, God cares about what we have to say. He "accepts" our prayers, as Psalm 6:9 says. Humbling and amazing.

In fact, it was this very passage that broke through to my friend Mary. Her therapist—a Christian—had given her a number of passages to reflect on, ones in which God hears his people. Psalm 6:6 resonated with her because she was in despair when she went to God. Reading that God not only heard her cries but accepted what she had to say changed her whole attitude about being heard.

While it didn't cure her clinical depression, it did help Mary realize that if God heard and accepted what she had to say, then so should others. Mary became more confident in expressing herself—stopped saying things in a small voice but instead spoke with confidence, assuming others *would* listen. Would hear her. And it made a huge difference.

Response

God, thank you for hearing me when I call out to you. And thank you for not just listening to my praises and thanksgiving but for hearing me out when I get whiny or frustrated or angry. Help me now to listen for you.

What does God say? See Psalm 40:1.

You Are Protected

Psalm 31:1–3

In you, LORD, I have taken refuge;
    let me never be put to shame;
    deliver me in your righteousness.
Turn your ear to me,
    come quickly to my rescue;
be my rock of refuge,
    a strong fortress to save me.
Since you are my rock and my fortress,
    for the sake of your name lead and guide me.

I had been prepared for many of the emotions I'd feel as a new mom. I was ready for the rush of love when it hit, though as my mother warned me it would, it did take a couple of days to come. I was ready for my nurturing instinct to kick in, even though I'd never been a "baby person" before. I was ready for the selflessness, even though I'd always been rather selfish.

But I wasn't ready for the fierce protectiveness I felt for my son, even though I'd been a fiercely protective and loyal person my whole life. I was not prepared for the "mama bear" emotions that would arise whenever I felt anyone was a threat to my child. And I wasn't prepared for how many potential threats would surround my family. While some of these threats I could protect my baby from (I could childproof, lock doors, change batteries in smoke detectors, use car seats, put on life vests, and on and on), I wasn't prepared for how many of the threats against my kids I had so little control over.

In fact, it's easy to get overwhelmed with all the dangers that lurk in this world, all the dangers we cannot protect our kids from. And it's easy for us mama bears to fret over how little control we actually have.

What I've learned, however, is that the way God equipped us to protect our children—vigilantly, tirelessly—is yet another way we mirror God. While we may never be able to perfectly protect our children, God is always our protector.

Of course, in this broken world, this doesn't mean that we—or our kids—will never suffer harm. It doesn't mean that we won't have to walk through scary times, that we won't have to endure times of uncertainty and insecurity. In John 16:33, Jesus tells us himself that in this world we *will* have trouble. It's a given.

So, it's not that God's protection means that we will never be harmed in any way. But what it does mean is what Jesus tells us just after promising us trouble: that he has overcome the world. It's a truth the psalmist was recognizing in this passage. When hard times do befall us, when we do get hurt, we can take refuge in the One who has overcome it all.

Response

God, while I don't understand why you allow so many fearful things to happen in this world, and while I wish you would simply zap all of life's monsters, I cling to the truth that you hold me in your mighty hand. I am safe in your strong grip.

What does God say? See John 10:27–29.

PART 3

You Are Part of God's Story

Praise the LORD.

Praise the LORD from the heavens;
    praise him in the heights above.
Praise him, all his angels;
    praise him, all his heavenly hosts.
Praise him, sun and moon;
    praise him, all you shining stars.
Praise him, you highest heavens
    and you waters above the skies.

Let them praise the name of the LORD,
    for at his command they were created,
and he established them for ever and ever—
    he issued a decree that will never pass away.

Praise the LORD from the earth,
    you great sea creatures and all ocean depths,
lightning and hail, snow and clouds,
    stormy winds that do his bidding,
you mountains and all hills,
    fruit trees and all cedars,
wild animals and all cattle,
    small creatures and flying birds,

kings of the earth and all nations,
    you princes and all rulers on earth,
young men and women,
    old men and children.

Let them praise the name of the Lord,
    for his name alone is exalted;
    his splendor is above the earth and the heavens.
And he has raised up for his people a horn,
    the praise of all his faithful servants,
    of Israel, the people close to his heart.

Praise the Lord.

Psalm 148

You Are a Storyteller

Psalm 71:15

> My mouth will tell of your righteous deeds,
>   of your saving acts all day long—
>   though I know not how to relate them all.

When I was little, my mother would tell me stories from her own—
often harrowing—childhood. I loved hearing my mom tell me about
the time her cat dashed under her bed and came out with a "huge
river rat" between its jaws. And I loved the stories about the muddy
river that ran behind her house that would flood and about how
the water moccasins would slither up into the pine trees and hang
from the boughs.

My favorite stories were my mother's worst memories. While
this seems horrible at surface value, I loved these stories because
they offered excitement and a view into a world I didn't understand
(and a life very different from the one I was living). Also, in these
stories my mother was a bona fide hero: a girl who survived having
a river rat *under her bed* and who lived to tell having seen snakes
dangling from her trees.

For me these two stories in particular shed so much light on
who my mother was and who she became. I knew my mom better
through her stories.

This is what hearing each other's stories can do for us; the stories offer glimpses into new or different worlds and offer deeper views of who we are.

While stories of rats under beds and snakes in trees may not seem like stories with deep theological meaning—and like the psalmist, my mother didn't know exactly how to "relate" them to me as a young girl—I learned from my mom's stories what it meant to face down fears. And about how God is with us, even in the scariest of times. How God can give us courage to deal with circumstances that seem beyond our control.

And I learned that God can take the terrifying circumstances and redeem them. My mother didn't even need to utter the word *God* for me to see that he had worked something mighty in her life by taking situations that scared her once upon a time and turning them into stories she could now giggle about as she told—and exaggerated—them, all to delight her little girl.

We can see God in our stories. Which is why we're called to be *storytellers*. To tell others the stories of our lives—about the things we've endured and survived, the areas where we've failed and succeeded, and the times we've questioned and doubted. Because in all of these stories, others can see what God has done for us. And we can see it too.

Response

Thank you, God, for being so at work in my life. And thank you for all the stories you've given me to tell—of the ways you've "shown up," of the ways you've revealed your goodness and your healing power. Help me to share these stories boldly with a world that needs to hear them.

What does God say? See Psalm 111.

You Are a Conduit of Faithfulness

Psalm 100:5

For the LORD is good and his love endures forever;
his faithfulness continues through all generations.

When my kids' school celebrated one hundred years of Christian education, Psalm 100:5 was the celebration theme. The Lord is good—and had been good to this school. His loving hand had been upon the school and its students, faculty, staff, and parents. And his faithfulness could be seen in the generations of children who had attended the school.

As part of the celebration, I wrote a history of the school and its community for the school's alumni magazine. I spent hours sifting through school archives, news clippings, and photos—of the first graduating class, of the prim students from the 1940s and 1950s to the increasingly shaggy students of the 1960s and 1970s and to the big-banged girls of my own era in the 1980s.

I laughed and smiled my way through many of these photos and stories. I had expected to do that. What I didn't expect was the *emotion* that rose in me and brought tears to my eyes. In everything I saw and read—from 1911 through 2011—God's faithfulness wafted up from the pages. It wasn't that the things I read or the pictures I saw were perfect or that the lives in them were lived without difficulty, but these relics from the past testified to God's presence and his enduring love for his people through the ages.

Has this happened to you while looking through old family photos or reading the journals of those long gone? Have you been struck by evidence of God's faithfulness to your own family, perhaps?

I know that even with ancestors of mine who didn't acknowledge God or weren't particularly "tight" with Jesus, I've been able to sense God's presence working through my family history. And I love that. I love knowing that he's been intertwined in the lives of everyone in my family tree, whether or not they acknowledged it. God has been faithful to my family through the generations— through good times and bad, through birth and death, through illness and healing. God's been good and loving and faithful.

One of the most exciting roles we have as moms is that we get to be "conduits" of this faithfulness. We get to pass down to another generation the stories we heard growing up and stories about what we've experienced that illustrate God's faithfulness to our family.

In many ways, this is exactly what the Bible offers us—a glimpse into God's hand throughout human history. And when we pass down our own stories and the biblical story to the next generation, we continue that saga.

Response

God, thank you for your great faithfulness to me and to my family. Thank you for being faithful to us even when we are not faithful to you. For showing signs of your goodness every day. Help me pass these stories to my children so that future generations will know of your unfailing love.

What does God say? See Lamentations 3.

You Are a Voice in the Chorus

Psalm 148:7–12

Praise the LORD from the earth,
    you great sea creatures and all ocean depths,
lightning and hail, snow and clouds,
    stormy winds that do his bidding,
you mountains and all hills,
    fruit trees and all cedars,
wild animals and all cattle,
    small creatures and flying birds,
kings of the earth and all nations,
    you princes and all rulers on earth,
young men and women,
    old men and children.

My kids like to cloud-gaze, but not while lying on their backs on the crisp lawn. They love to do it from our dining room table. On days when the skies shine blue but are ruffled with clouds, my kids will often look out the big picture window in our dining room and call out what they see in the passing clouds.

They'll start with some usual cloud suspects: the bunnies, the floppy-eared dogs, the clown heads. Then they'll get punchy and start seeing potty-humor shapes throughout the heavens. It was when this happened last week that I attempted to rein in the gross-out level a bit by asking a weird question: "Did you ever think that maybe God's on the other side of the sky? Watching the clouds drift and switch shapes too?"

This stopped the potty humor for all of two seconds. They all shrugged their "Yeah, cools" but went back to cracking each other up.

The thought, however, led me to another: that these clouds, masses of white gas floating through the atmosphere, praise God. And that when we humans sing or write or pray out our praises, ours are just one of many, many "voices" shooting up from earth to the heavens.

In some ways, this seems overwhelming—like our voices may be drowned out by those of the animals, the lightning, the trees, the "stormy winds," as the psalmist calls them. But that day I found huge comfort knowing I was one of these voices, that all God's creatures and all of God's creation *praise* him. Each of us in our own way. Each of us using what we've got, as an offering to God.

The clouds can give God their movement, their shapes. The sea creatures may offer their dives or sleek swims. Lions can offer their roars; cheetahs their races. Trees offer their reach and sways; storms offer their flashes and booms.

And us? We can offer what we've got. Some days that may be more than others. But every day we can find ways to offer God our words, our movement, our tears, our smiles. Our very lives. All add to the beautiful chorus of praise rising up to the heavens.

Response

God, some days my house gets so loud with the sounds of family life I can barely hear myself think. And yet, with all the sounds rising up from this earth, you can still hear me. Thank you for hearing my single voice as well as letting me be part of this great and beautiful chorus of praise.

What does God say? See 1 Chronicles 16:30–34.

You Are a Valuable Player

Psalm 68:24–25

Your procession, God, has come into view,
    the procession of my God and King into the sanctuary.
In front are the singers, after them the musicians;
    with them are the young women playing the timbrels.

When I was probably twelve, my friend and I had a long conversation about what life would be like if we were singers. Would we rather—one of us had asked—have a solo career or would we rather front a band? That is, would we rather be Madonna (name alone in lights) or be in the Go-Go's (one member of a group)?

I didn't waver in my answer: I'd be in the band. Going solo seemed like a heavy burden, a lonely life. Even if you didn't have to split the profits quite as much.

So it comes as no surprise to me that in my life as a writer (the singing life was never meant to be), I've sought out ways to be a part of a "band." Though for the most part my name appears by itself on article bylines and book covers, I am part of a larger collection of writers.

In fact, when my friend emailed me years ago to see if I'd like to start up a writers' group with her, I jumped at the chance—as if I were once again twelve. Unwavering in my answer, I wanted to be part of the band, a valuable player in a larger group.

I've long wondered about this part of my personality, what it is that makes me long so deeply for the community, that makes me so uncomfortable when it's "just me" out there. I'm pretty sure this is simply part of human nature—the longing we all have to *belong*, to be part of something bigger than ourselves. Even if we have to do many of the tasks in life all by ourselves.

It's certainly this way with motherhood, and it's the reason many of us love heading to MOPS groups. We may be the "solo act" when it comes to mothering our kids, but it sure is nice to know we have a group of fellow mothers ready to back us from time to time.

This is just the way God made us, I believe. We were made to be in community, to be a part of something bigger than ourselves.

But being a part of that community doesn't mean who God made us to be gets lost in the crowd. Each of us has an essential role to play—we are valuable players! That community we all long for should be the place that encourages us, emboldens us, and equips us to get back out there and face the crowds of life—even when we have to do it alone.

Response

God, I want to believe I can do everything on my own, but I know I can't. I know that a life dependent on you and on others is the way you meant us to live. But sometimes it's hard to find community I can trust and that I can rely on. Bring people into my life who can help support me and help me live as you made me—and whom I can help as well. And help me get rid of my "I can do it all" attitude and know that you are the only One who can do it all.

What does God say? See Matthew 28:20.

You Are Crucial to the Plot

Psalm 86:16

Turn to me and have mercy on me;
    show your strength in behalf of your servant;
save me, because I serve you
    just as my mother did.

Read through the Old Testament and you'll notice something: dads get a lot of the glory. Moms? Not so much. Of course, the ancient Jewish (as well as broader) culture of the Old Testament was patriarchal, so this makes sense. Back then, men mattered much more than women; boys much more than girls.

But the truth is that God has never thought of women or moms or daughters or sisters as *lesser*. Women have always played a central, leading role in the story of God's love for and redemption of his people.

We see this clearly when Jesus entered the picture. God called a young girl to the greatest role in all of human history: to be the mother to God's only begotten Son. We see it in the way Jesus interacted with women during his time on earth. Jesus included women where society excluded them. We see God's heart for women when Paul declares that in Christ "there is neither Jew nor Gentile, neither slave nor free, nor is there male and female, for you are all one in Christ Jesus" (Gal. 3:28).

These were jarring words to a polarized society. And yet, even in this world, a mother's influence on her children was understood. Certainly David understood the connection between his own faith and that of his mother. In Psalm 86:16, he appeals to God to save him, to have mercy on him not only because of his own service to God but because of his mama's. What a testimony!

Our faith—our journey with God—isn't just crucial to our own lives. It's crucial to the entire story of God and us. How we live, how we love, how we seek God even in the darkest times matters far beyond ourselves. It affects our kids and their kids and everyone they reach.

Thousands of years after David wrote these words, we're still reading and clinging to them. Words that came out of his own desperation and words that connected right back to the influence of his mother. While we don't hear much about David's mom in the Old Testament, she is a crucial player, a key part of his and God's and *our* story.

Response

God, some days being a mom seems so insignificant. But I know you see this role differently. Help me to see that my everyday, nitty-gritty, down-in-the-dirt role as a mom is crucial to the plot of your grand story. Help me teach my kids things about you that will be bound around their hearts and that will guide them as they walk through life.

What does God say? See Proverbs 6:20–22.

PART 4

You Are a Work in Progress

Of David.

In you, Lord my God,
  I put my trust.

I trust in you;
    do not let me be put to shame,
    nor let my enemies triumph over me.
No one who hopes in you
    will ever be put to shame,
but shame will come on those
    who are treacherous without cause.

Show me your ways, Lord,
    teach me your paths.
Guide me in your truth and teach me,
    for you are God my Savior,
    and my hope is in you all day long.
Remember, Lord, your great mercy and love,
    for they are from of old.
Do not remember the sins of my youth
    and my rebellious ways;
according to your love remember me,
    for you, Lord, are good.

Good and upright is the LORD;
    therefore he instructs sinners in his ways.
He guides the humble in what is right
    and teaches them his way.
All the ways of the LORD are loving and faithful
    toward those who keep the demands of his covenant.
For the sake of your name, LORD,
    forgive my iniquity, though it is great.

Who, then, are those who fear the LORD?
    He will instruct them in the ways they should choose.
They will spend their days in prosperity,
    and their descendants will inherit the land.
The LORD confides in those who fear him;
    he makes his covenant known to them.
My eyes are ever on the LORD,
    for only he will release my feet from the snare.

Turn to me and be gracious to me,
    for I am lonely and afflicted.
Relieve the troubles of my heart
    and free me from my anguish.
Look on my affliction and my distress
    and take away all my sins.
See how numerous are my enemies
    and how fiercely they hate me!

Guard my life and rescue me;
    do not let me be put to shame,
    for I take refuge in you.
May integrity and uprightness protect me,
    because my hope, LORD, is in you.

Deliver Israel, O God,
    from all their troubles!

                                       Psalm 25

You Are Refined by Motherhood

Psalm 127:1–2

Unless the LORD builds the house,
  the builders labor in vain.
Unless the LORD watches over the city,
  the guards stand watch in vain.
In vain you rise early
  and stay up late,
toiling for food to eat—
  for he grants sleep to those he loves.

When I was in the throes of my (first) identity crisis as a mom, I refused to admit that motherhood had changed me at all. I would steadfastly affirm that I was the same exact person post-kids as I was pre-kids.

Of course, this was silly. And wrong. Motherhood *did* change me. It changed you too. None of us are exactly the same as we were before we had kids. But the changes that occur are not in ways many of us expect—especially when we're knee-deep in wondering who we are now that we are mothers.

The changes that occur in motherhood are less about removing the very core of who we are and replacing it with something—or someone—new than they are about refinement, about smoothing out, expanding, compressing.

To put it into the terms of today's Scripture, the changes are more about a sturdy home remodel than a complete demolition and totally new construction. Sometimes it may take getting right down to the foundation—but this allows us to build our lives on the foundation of God and the roles and gifts and passions and personalities he gave us.

In many ways, I believe God has used motherhood as a time to remodel—and in some parts rebuild—who I was, especially the parts of me that had been built "in vain."

God has used motherhood to show me the areas of my life that needed work or to be torn down—my problems with worry and materialism, for instance. But motherhood has also been a time of expansion; it seems that my heart added all kinds of rooms to hold the love that motherhood has brought my way, for example.

But beyond even the emotions, God uses motherhood to firm up who we are, who he created us to be, as it brings into focus what really matters in our lives and what doesn't. Motherhood has taught me that I *need* time to myself, time to read and to write, time to simply sit quietly with God, if I am going to be a good mom. And that that is okay. Where once upon a time I felt guilty or bad for needing this alone space, for needing to express my "non-mom gifts," now I understand that it's how God made me. The demands of motherhood have taught me this.

Friends of mine have experienced this differently; they never realized how much they needed the company of good friends to help them find sanity at the end of crazy weeks. And that this is okay. Not selfish. Instead, the way God made them.

Many of us must admit that much of our lives have been built on pretty flimsy ideas of what makes a "good" life. Many of the things we have filled our lives with are based on what our culture or families or friends say we need to fill them with. So we have spent time doing things that may not be *sinful* but aren't what God has for us. Which means they are in vain.

Motherhood offers a wonderful time to take stock of our lives—of the ways we spend our days and with whom we're spending them—and seek God. To ask him to show us if our lives are being lived or built as he would have them or if there are ways he can offer us a rebuild or at least a good scrub so we can rest easy—just as this passage says—in the way God made us and in his love.

Response

God, on so many days I'm tempted to follow what the "world" says is best for me and my family. I want to believe the advertisements and what others tell me I "need" for a good life. And yet, I know that's not always what you say is best. Help me instead to build my life and my family on your "rock"—on your words, your truth, and your plan.

What does God say? See Matthew 7:24–27.

You Are Shaped by Experience

Psalm 78:2–4

I will open my mouth with a parable;
    I will utter hidden things, things from of old—
things we have heard and known,
    things our ancestors have told us.
We will not hide them from their descendants;
    we will tell the next generation
the praiseworthy deeds of the LORD,
    his power, and the wonders he has done.

Just before my first child, Henrik, was born, my mom asked me a question: "Have you ever felt like I didn't love you?"

I told her no. I always knew she loved me.

Well, she went on. She didn't actually *always* love me. "It took a while for the full love to kick in. A couple of days, maybe."

She told me this not to make me feel bad (strangely, I didn't) but so that I wouldn't feel bad if that rush of love didn't hit me immediately.

I've been forever grateful for her words. Especially since the rush of love *didn't* hit me right away. It did take a couple of days—at least for my first two children—for me to fall head over heels, for the near-maniacal levels of fierce, protective, unrelenting, unconditional love to pulse through my veins.

If my mother hadn't shared her own experience with me, if she hadn't been willing to pass on what she knew to be true, I might have been left a mess, sunk by guilt, and wondering what was wrong with me as a mother those first couple of days when "love" wasn't the forefront emotion. I might have felt this way, much as I suspect my mom felt this way.

But my mom—thank God—made an important choice. Instead of letting something like "I didn't love my baby for two days!" become shameful and hidden and regaled to the annals of "never tell a soul," she allowed her experience of pain and of worry and of guilt to *shape* her and then to help me.

Which is just what today's psalm talks about.

We all experience circumstances or do things or say words we'd love to forget, things we'd rather keep hidden and buried. And yet, what good does that do? Especially when we look back on those things and see how God has worked in them, how he has used a negative and turned it into a positive. When we see how our lives have been shaped by those very things.

Consider my mom's love for me. She may not have been the sort to declare, "I've loved you ever since I first found I was pregnant," but I've never once felt unloved by my mom. Not every daughter can say that.

Even choosing to tell me about her days of guilt and shame and wondering what was wrong with her is a sign of her love. She was willing to put forward what others might have hidden—because of her love for me. Well, and her love for God. Because my mom permitted herself to be shaped by motherhood and by her relationship with God, allowing bringing me into the world, raising me, and loving me to be a great work of God in her life, a testament to how far she could come. And her telling me the stories that others might have kept hidden became praise to God as well.

Response

God, I've spent too much time feeling lost in guilt and shame. Please forgive me for the things I've done wrong to cause that guilt, but also help me accept your gift of grace. Help me pass on this gift to my kids as well. Let me raise them to know that mistakes are not the end-all, but that with you at work in our lives, there is hope and grace and a million second chances.

What does God say? See Psalm 145:3–5.

You Are Led by God

Psalm 25:4–5

Show me your ways, LORD,
    teach me your paths.
Guide me in your truth and teach me,
    for you are God my Savior,
    and my hope is in you all day long.

My friend Ann looked at me from across the table and took a deep breath. "I just have no idea what I'm supposed to do," she said.

Ann had left full-time employment not long after her first child was born to join the ranks of the freelance work-from-home moms. This worked out perfectly until the day her husband lost his job, and the months of his looking for work dragged on until she realized she, too, should be sending out résumés, looking for full-time, benefit-providing work.

I ran into her at a coffee shop the day after she got a job offer for a position that paid well but would take her out of the life she had come to know and love and into a new season of ten-hour work days away from her little girls.

Ann was excited about the opportunity to be able to provide for her family, but angry that God had allowed this turn of events in her life. It made no sense why she was being called to end her "good thing going," as she called it, to trade it in for a life that seemed "less than."

I didn't have any answers. I have no idea why sometimes God flips life on its head, why he allows bad things to happen, or why he leads us places we don't want to go.

This is one of the reasons I love digging into the psalms. The psalmists, no matter how smart and talented and often insightful they were, seemed to wrestle with these same ideas. People have been wrestling with this—wondering about this—for ages.

While we don't know the *whys* of life, we do know the *Who*. We know that no matter where life takes us, God is with us. We know that wherever God leads, he's got us by the hand. We know that whatever confusing or even treacherous path we may need to traverse, God lights each step.

Sometimes this isn't what we want to hear. Even those of us who love God and seek to follow him. Ann would rather have heard that God would restore her old life, send her husband the job, because following God—even if he was with her, lighting her steps and holding her hand—wasn't easy.

But through the fulfillment Ann got from work and the gift of time her husband now had with their girls, she discovered it was worth it. Following God and his path—whatever that is—is always worth it.

Response

God, I long for clear road signs, for well-lit paths and a detailed map. But life's roads are so confusing. Please guide me. Help me trust that while I may not be able to see the full route, you do lead the way. And your words are lamps for my steps.

What does God say? See Psalm 119:105.

You Are Affected by Choices

> I have sought your face with all my heart;
> be gracious to me according to your promise.
> I have considered my ways
> and have turned my steps to your statutes.

I don't often get chills while watching TV—certainly not the sort of chills that convict me. But during one episode of *Downton Abbey*, Lady Mary, the eldest daughter character, shows little sympathy for one of their maids, who ends up pregnant out of wedlock and totally out of luck.

When Lady Mary's sister accuses her of being rather harsh toward the maid, Mary asks, "Why? Aren't we all stuck with the choices we make?"

If you know the show, you know these are powerful words from her, as she's made some agonizing—and often downright wrong—choices that she is indeed stuck with, that have affected nearly every other area of her life.

My chills and conviction came in connection with my own acknowledgment of choices and decisions I had made in my life that seemed to be coming home to roost in my family life. Nothing huge. Nothing horrible. But still enough to make me realize perhaps some of the difficulty I was living with wasn't God's punishment or anyone else's fault, but simply a result of my own poor choices.

Though there isn't agreement on who wrote Psalm 119, many scholars believe it was David. David knew a thing or two about poor choices. Though God loved him and chose him for great things and though he loved God and sought to do God's will, David was a man who chose badly. The book of 2 Samuel is full of stories of his choices gone wrong.

And yet, David also knew a thing or two about how God can redeem and transform even the poorest choices and how God is always there, just a few steps away from our poor choices, offering us help to get back on the right path—God's path.

This is wonderful news for us, but especially comforting to us as moms who make mistakes every day. We may have to live with the consequences of poor choices, but we also have a God who is ready to forgive us, to welcome us as we turn our steps back to God's statutes—as the psalm says—and to turn what may seem like curses into blessings. And this is the best way our choices—even our poor choices—can affect us.

Response

God, I've made so many mistakes—as a child, as a woman, now as a mother. But even as I live with the consequences of those actions, I know that you love me, you forgive me, and you can use anything for ultimate good. Help me to learn and grow from my mistakes—and to model that for my children. Thank you for your grace and your mercy in my life.

What does God say? See Romans 5:8.

You Are Influenced by Culture

Psalm 44:1

We have heard it with our ears, O God;
   our ancestors have told us
what you did in their days,
   in days long ago.

One of my friends likes to say that our culture is heading down-hill in a hurry—that our moral compass is off, that we've lost our collective focus on God, and that the world has never been worse. My friend claims it's never been harder to raise our kids with Christian values.

While certainly there are aspects of this culture that don't align with Judeo-Christian values—some lyrics in popular music and the prevalence of human sex trafficking come to mind—I don't agree with my friend. After all, it only takes a quick look back at human history, back to the days of legalized slavery and then segregation, to see that the world has always been a broken mess. Full of moral depravity and sketchiness, full of people who seek their own interest at all and any cost, people who fail to seek God. Our culture has always presented challenges to parents because there have always been forces that worked against the good we try to teach our kids.

And yet, the world has also always been filled with good things—good things that coexist along with the bad, good things that come out of the bad, and good things that shine so brightly that they nearly blur the bad into oblivion.

What's important is not whether the world is worse or better, but that we recognize the good and the bad in our culture and that we know we are influenced by it all—by the good, the bad, and even the neutral.

No matter how engaged or separated we are with culture, it influences us. Just as our parents' and grandparents' cultures influenced them. We are products—at least partly—of the world we live in. And we need to be able to identify the ways our culture may be at odds with what we want to teach our kids or what we may want to be ourselves. But we also need to be able to identify the good—and the ways God is at work—in our culture.

No matter how bad things may seem, God is indeed at work. Today's psalm speaks to this. "We have heard it with our ears, O God; our ancestors have told us what you did in their days, in days long ago." What God did in those days was to work within people groups, within cultures. And those are the stories the psalmists' ancestors passed on—the stories of God stepping in, maybe punishing misdeeds or maybe showing great mercy. Either way it was God transforming lives and changing hearts throughout influential cultures.

Response

God, this world can be a scary place. Not just the outright violence and evil, but the ways this culture can draw us away from you. When I worry about losing focus on you, help me see you in this world, in this culture. Help me to remember that this is your world and that you have not only overcome it, but that you reign above it.

What does God say? See John 16:33.

PART 5

You Are Made in God's Image

Praise the LORD.

I will extol the LORD with all my heart
  in the council of the upright and in the assembly.

Great are the works of the LORD;
  they are pondered by all who delight in them.
Glorious and majestic are his deeds,
  and his righteousness endures forever.
He has caused his wonders to be remembered;
  the LORD is gracious and compassionate.
He provides food for those who fear him;
  he remembers his covenant forever.

He has shown his people the power of his works,
  giving them the lands of other nations.
The works of his hands are faithful and just;
  all his precepts are trustworthy.
They are established for ever and ever,
  enacted in faithfulness and uprightness.
He provided redemption for his people;
  he ordained his covenant forever—
  holy and awesome is his name.

The fear of the LORD is the beginning of wisdom;
all who follow his precepts have good understanding.
To him belongs eternal praise.

Psalm 111

You Are the Work of God's Hands

Psalm 103:13–14

As a father has compassion on his children,
    so the LORD has compassion on those who fear him;
for he knows how we are formed,
    he remembers that we are dust.

Last week, one of my kids—whom I'll call "Pat" to avoid embarrassment—had a major, age-*in*appropriate meltdown. The kind of meltdown to end all meltdowns. The kind you hoped your kids had left behind at age two, but that seems to rear its ugly, melty head every now and again.

It all started when I asked Pat to do something this child did *not* "feel like" doing, and when I pressed that it didn't matter how one felt, Pat let me know through tears and yelling and arm waving all the reasons this task would not be happening.

When my husband, Rafi, came into the room mid-meltdown, he looked at me like I was out of my mind, wondering why I was letting this go on. I suppose I let it go on because I *understood* why Pat was melting down. I understood Pat's meltdown because I'm known to do the same—well, not *exactly* the same—when I am tired and in need of a snack. I know full well what it's like to get to that point where I'm so worn down and hungry that even the tiniest request of me sends me over the edge. My child is very much like me in this regard. Pat is wonderfully natured until sleepiness or hunger strikes.

So while plenty might argue that a good sending-to-the-room would've been appropriate, in this moment I let my understanding of my child's "condition" lead me away from discipline and toward compassion. (Besides, I had allowed my child to become overtired and overhungry, so it seemed silly to punish the problem instead of solve it!) And I like to think this response is similar to one God has offered me time and again.

While certainly God does discipline us at times—and while certainly we are called to discipline our children—I love what today's verse tells us about God's compassion. It is because we are the works of God's own hands that God *knows* how we are formed, that he understands our limitations so well, that he shows his great compassion and mercy toward us.

Response

God, thank you for the way you allow your understanding of my humanity to fuel your compassionate heart. Please help me show that same merciful compassion toward others.

What does God say? See Isaiah 49:14–16.

You Are Loving

Psalm 119:41–42

May your unfailing love come to me, LORD,
  your salvation, according to your promise;
then I can answer anyone who taunts me,
  for I trust in your word.

Despite all the areas I fail at in mothering (I'm not a consistent disciplinarian; I'm prone to snapping or yelling when I get tired; and I still have no good organization system for toys), I excel at loving my children.

I am good at feeling love and showing them love. I frequently tell them I love them; I'm usually willing to drop everything for a snuggle; and I believe I have each of their "love languages" figured out so I can show them love in ways they will particularly understand.

Loving my kids comes easily. Naturally. While at times I find them aggravating or hurtful, I can't imagine anything that could make me stop loving my children. I can't conceive of anything any one of them could do—no matter how heinous—that would cause my love to end.

It's inconceivable. With rare exception, a mother's love is integrated so deep within her being that there is no removing it, there's no lessening it. It's a miraculous force, as this is something that perhaps more than anything else reflects the image of God in our lives.

We love deeply, strongly, passionately, and fiercely because God loves us these same ways. We love because we are made in the image of a God whose love for us cannot and will not run out or fade away. We love because God made us like him in this way—to love. And the wonderful thing about love is that it benefits the giver as well as the recipient.

Just as the way we love our children helps them grow up secure and confident and ready and able to face this world, God's love provides that for us. "May your unfailing love come to me, LORD, your salvation," the psalmist writes, "then I can answer anyone who taunts me." It is through receiving God's *unfailing* love that the psalmist finds strength, finds ways to respond to bullies.

God's love is more than simply warm fuzzies and happy feelings; it's about equipping us. The same can be said for a mother's love, I believe. We love our children—unfailingly, unconditionally—because it's that love that helps them as they venture out into the world, that gives them confidence to do what they've been called to do, that lets them know that even when they fail they are still loved.

But our love for our kids does something else. When we show love and live out this wonderful reflection of God's image, we point our kids to the Giver of love, to God himself.

Response

God, thank you for giving me people to love. While I love imperfectly, help my love to become more like your love every day. Help me to love patiently and kindly. Help my love protect and trust and hope and persevere. Just as you love me.

What does God say? See 1 Corinthians 13.

You Are Creative

Psalm 19:1

The heavens declare the glory of God;
  the skies proclaim the work of his hands.

My mom makes amazing centerpieces. No matter what the occasion (formal or carefree), no matter the medium (beautiful flowers or old bingo cards), my mom can create pieces that turn that middle place of a table into a talking point for days.

My friend Kristi throws parties for her daughters that would shame Martha Stewart. The little guests come home from her house having had a wonderful time with friends, while making Kristi-designed T-shirts and clever crafts to commemorate the party.

My friend Betty assembles individualized road-trip activity kits for her four boys whenever they head out for the daylong drive to their grandmother's house. The boys stay busy for hours, keeping nagging and fighting at bay as they drive over some of the most boring, flat land the United States has to offer.

Other friends of mine play heart-moving piano. Some paint or concoct outdoor games at the drop of a hat. Still others have started their own businesses. Some have *invented* things. Many of my friends write.

I stand in awe of each of these women—at their gifts and abilities to *create*. But what's funny is that many of these women don't think much of their creative abilities at all. When praised, these women shrug and say, "Oh, it's nothing."

But it's not nothing. Our creative abilities—no matter what shape they take or how they are expressed—are some of the most important ways we reflect God.

After all, the very first thing we learn about God when reading the Scriptures, about who he is, is that he is creative.

"In the beginning God *created* the heavens and the earth," Genesis 1:1 tells us (emphasis mine). And the psalmist tells us that that very creation proclaims his glory and the work he can do. God is creative. He is a creator who paints the skies, who sculpts humans, who brings forth music from swamplands, who wrote a story of redemption for his people. All that proclaims God's glory and the work of his hands.

When we allow our creativity to flourish, when we bring our creative abilities and thoughts out from private realms and into the broader world, we too proclaim God's glory. This is because we are creative—and we are *all* creative—because God is creative. Because we are made in his image to create, to dream up, to bring forth, to proclaim glory.

Response

God, some days it's hard to imagine that I was made in your image. And yet, when I see my kids create art projects and dream up games, I see their creativity as a reflection of yours. Help me to tap into my own creative spirit as well. Help me to do this not so others may be amazed at my gifts, but so others can see a reflection of my Creator.

What does God say? See Genesis 1.

You Are Desirous of Good

Psalm 101:2

I will be careful to lead a blameless life—
   when will you come to me?
I will conduct the affairs of my house
   with a blameless heart.

I was tired. I was stressed. I was fed up. Never a good combination when it comes to discipline. So when my kids started fighting with one another—yet again—over who would get to hold the remote, I lost it. I stood up and started yelling at them. Pointing my finger and telling them how they were adding to an already bad day. How my first opportunity to relax all day was being ruined by their ridiculous bickering. How all I wanted was a little peace, a little quiet, and a little time to get lost in a TV show.

I kept yelling at my three kids as they each marched up the stairs to their rooms, where I had sent them all. I issued one final "argh!" and slapped my hand on the back of the sofa before I heard their doors close.

And then I remembered the look on my son's face as he said, "Sorry, Mama." I slouched down on the sofa and breathed out slowly. Once again, I had acted badly. I had done wrong. Even worse than the very thing I had just punished my kids for. They were in trouble for retaliating when they drove each other nuts—and yet here I sat, guilty of the same thing. In fact, they probably learned this from me.

I felt horrible. Just as I did every time I behaved badly as a mama. Sure, it was my job to discipline the kids when they acted out of line, my job to make sure they knew right from wrong and that there were consequences when they acted out, but it was not my job to yell unnecessarily, to react knee-jerk-ily, or to discipline unlovingly. And I had done all three.

Before I headed up the stairs to talk to—and apologize to—my kids, I prayed. Asking God for forgiveness. And asking that he help me be a *good* mom in all that I do—even in the hard tasks of discipline and even when I'm worn out, frustrated, and justifiably angry. Because almost more than anything, I long to be a good mom. Not a good mom as the world may define a good mom (think: bakes perfect cookies, throws perfect parties, vacuums in heels and pearls), but as *God* would define a good mom (think: the Golden Rule and love your neighbor).

And this desire—to *be* good, to *do* good to and for my kids—is yet another wonderful way we bear God's image. God, of course, is good. All the time, as we say. Even in the times when it feels that life isn't fair or that God's not hearing our prayers—or answering them in the way we'd want—God is good and wants the best for us. Just as we do for our kids.

Response

God, I long to do right by my family—and by you. I want to be a good mother and a good woman. I want to do good things in this world. But so often I fail. Please forgive me. And give me the tools I need to be that good mom and good woman I long to be.

What does God say? See Ephesians 2:10 and 1 John 1:9.

You Are Complex

Psalm 111:2–4

Great are the works of the LORD;
    they are pondered by all who delight in them.
Glorious and majestic are his deeds
    and his righteousness endures forever.
He has caused his wonders to be remembered.

When I'm speaking to various MOPS or mothers' groups across the country, I like to lead the moms in an identity exercise. It's based on something my dad used to ask interviewees when he worked in human resources. It's a simple set of questions: What did you want to be when you were seven? What makes you feel most alive? What does a great day look like to you? What do you do well naturally that other people don't? What do you dream of? What issues fire up your soul or break your heart? And so on.

I encourage the women to answer these questions boldly and honestly—not to answer what they think they *should* or even *wish* (no need to pretend that a great day is being alone with all the kids with nary a break!), but to answer in truth, without fear of seeming proud or braggy.

Then I encourage women to choose one word that describes each of their answers so they have an arsenal of words ready to be used to describe who they are. Words that can be tacked on to the end of the sentence *I am a mom and a* _____. Words that, when we feel that no one really knows us or that we don't know ourselves anymore, can be called up, relied upon to remind us who God made us to be.

And I want us to remember that we aren't just any *one* of these words, but *all of them*. We moms are complex creatures. Multi-faceted, in the image of God.

God—in his goodness—gave us so many words, so many images to let us know who he is. Throughout Scripture, God identifies himself as a rock, a fortress, as Abba Father, and even as a mother hen! God lets us see him as a spirit, and as a human—with Jesus. Jesus tells us that he is the Bread of Life; the Living Water; and the Way, the Truth, and the Life.

Throughout the stories in the Bible, we see God as a redeemer, a rescuer, a savior, a protector, and a provider. And on and on. The words and images for God are almost endless because God is complex. And it's important that we understand and get to know God as a complex being. This is why the psalmist writes of "pondering" the works of the Lord. Those of us who know God want to discover more about him!

And it's important that others get to know *us* that way as well. We are made—like God—to be many things, to have different passions and abilities and roles and relationships. These things all matter. To God, to our families, and to this world.

Response

God, sometimes I have no idea who I am any longer. I lose myself in a list of tasks and demands on my time. But you always know exactly who I am. And I am humbled by that. Thank you for not losing sight of me, even as I lose sight of myself. Help me to see myself—all my gifts and abilities and roles—just as you see me.

What does God say? See Psalm 8:5.

You Are Merciful

Psalm 82:1–4

God presides in the great assembly;
    he renders judgment among the "gods":
"How long will you defend the unjust
    and show partiality to the wicked?
Defend the weak and the fatherless;
    uphold the cause of the poor and the oppressed.
Rescue the weak and the needy;
    deliver them from the hand of the wicked."

It was sometime mid-prayer that it hit me. As I offered up some desperate words to God—that his hand would provide for our family in a rather dire financial situation, that he would protect my children from the stress the financial crisis brought our family, and that he would carry my family through this valley—I thought of the other mothers in my community and across the globe who cried these same things to God. And my heart broke.

I thought of the women who knew desperation I probably never would. While I prayed for relief from our difficulty, in truth, even our dire situation wouldn't be a matter of life and death. My kids would still eat. We would always have a warm place to sleep—even if it were in my in-laws' basement. We had people to help us in a pinch. In other words, as I prayed for God's provision, I was able to imagine so many ways he could provide. I realize not every mother enjoys that same broad imagination.

So I began to change my prayers. Although I continued to pray for our own financial relief, I added to my prayer—on a more consistent basis—the mothers who truly had no idea from whom their help would come. Who could hardly imagine the ways that even a big God could save them. And my heart continued to break every time I prayed this.

One of the best things motherhood has done for me is broaden my heart. Have you felt this too? It seems impossible now to *not* care about the welfare and livelihood of all kids once you've loved your own kids. For me, this love has meant a change in heart on some "social" issues, a change in the organizations I support, and a big change in prayer life. For some of my friends, this broadening of the heart has meant becoming activists—petitioning Congress and writing articles to raise awareness.

No matter what our broadened hearts compel us to do, it's wonderful to remember that this is yet another beautiful way we reflect God in our motherhood. Motherhood makes us more *merciful*. The love God puts in our hearts isn't meant for our children alone. We're given that immense love so we will stand up for the weak, the poor, and the oppressed, as today's psalm tells us. We do this because this is what God does for us.

Response

God, having children and becoming a mom has helped me understand the depths of your love for all your children. Help me to stay mindful of the needs of your children—and not just my own. Light fires of compassion and justice in my heart and soul, and let me be an instrument to help let your goodness and mercy roll throughout the world.

What does God say? See Amos 5:24.

PART 6

You Are Made for Many Things

For the director of music. For Jeduthun. A psalm of David.

I said, "I will watch my ways
    and keep my tongue from sin;
I will put a muzzle on my mouth
    while in the presence of the wicked."
So I remained utterly silent,
    not even saying anything good.
But my anguish increased;
    my heart grew hot within me.
While I meditated, the fire burned;
    then I spoke with my tongue:

"Show me, LORD, my life's end
    and the number of my days;
    let me know how fleeting my life is.
You have made my days a mere handbreadth;
    the span of my years is as nothing before you.
Everyone is but a breath,
    even those who seem secure.

"Surely everyone goes around like a mere phantom;
    in vain they rush about, heaping up wealth
    without knowing whose it will finally be.

"But now, LORD, what do I look for?
    My hope is in you.
Save me from all my transgressions;
    do not make me the scorn of fools.
I was silent; I would not open my mouth,
    for you are the one who has done this.
Remove your scourge from me;
    I am overcome by the blow of your hand.
When you rebuke and discipline anyone for their sin,
    you consume their wealth like a moth—
    surely everyone is but a breath.

"Hear my prayer, LORD,
    listen to my cry for help;
    do not be deaf to my weeping.
I dwell with you as a foreigner,
    a stranger, as all my ancestors were.
Look away from me, that I may enjoy life again
    before I depart and am no more."

Psalm 39

You Are Made to Live Your Gifts

Psalm 92:1–3

> It is good to praise the LORD
> and make music to your name, O Most High,
> proclaiming your love in the morning
> and your faithfulness at night,
> to the music of the ten-stringed lyre
> and the melody of the harp.

This is going to sound terrible, but sometimes I wish the psalmist David hadn't been a musician too. Because then, when we read words like the ones we read today, it wouldn't reinforce the idea that there are only certain ways to worship. You know what I mean here?

When we read that "it is good to praise the LORD and make music to your name" or when we read about proclaiming God's love to "the music of the ten-stringed lyre and the melody of the harp," we nod along. Of course music can do that. Anyone who's ever been to church can testify that music is almost always used in conjunction with praising God and proclaiming God's faithfulness and love.

But what does this say to those of us who aren't particularly musical? How are those of us who fear we'd make God tumble back off his throne if he heard us try to strike up a tune supposed to feel when we read these words?

We're supposed to feel just fine.

Although music is certainly one of the more common expressions of *public* worship, it is a far cry from being the only way God can be glorified and praised. In fact, God was praised by David's tending sheep, by his leading a nation, and by his love for his children as much as he was David's musicianship. Simply because God is praised when we live our gifts, when we use the talents and abilities God created us with. Anytime we do what we were made to do, we can do it to God's glory. We can worship through our gifts.

It's an amazing thing. But this attaches a whole other level of loss when we go through times when we feel we aren't able to live out our gifts because of the demands of motherhood, when we aren't able to find time or space to *do* the things we love to do and that we are made to do.

But the good news is that even when we can't be living out and praising God with certain gifts and abilities—or even our *main* gifts or abilities—being moms means we live lives replete with opportunities to praise God, to worship. Everything we do—every sandwich we make, every chocolate milk we stir, every little body we hug, every cheer we give—is an act of worship. Just as every client we represent, every wall we paint, every child we teach, every patient we see, every tennis ball we hit, every piano we play, or every gift we *use* can be worshipful.

The key is recognizing the One who gives us our gifts and abilities and opportunities and using them to the best of our ability to his glory.

We were made to live our gifts to honor God.

Response

God, before kids, it seemed easier to use my gifts for your glory. I had time! Even though I don't feel like I'm able to "live my gifts" as much as I like, God, I offer what I can do and all that you created me to do as a gift right back to you.

What does God say? See Colossians 3:17.

You Are Made to Flourish

Psalm 52:8

> But I am like an olive tree
> flourishing in the house of God;
> I trust in God's unfailing love
> for ever and ever.

"I'm just so tired," my friend whispered, her heavy eyes meeting mine. "It's like I might just wither away."

I smiled back at her and the newborn she held. "I remember that feeling," I said. "But it gets better. I promise."

What I failed to tell her at the time was that although sleep schedules eventually straighten out and it becomes once again possible to sleep more than two hours at a time, the truth was that I didn't need to go all the way back to the newborn days to remember feeling so worn down that I worried I would wither away. I pretty much just had to go back to the day before.

From what I gather, the tiredness that comes with being a mom just takes different shapes through the years. The newborn days wear us down by lack of REM sleep. The toddler and preschool years by all the chasing, all the playing, all the needs-meeting. The grade school years bring the worry of school and friends and kids who don't go to bed as early as they used to. And the high school and college years? I don't even want to think about that.

Each stage of motherhood has elements and challenges that can wear us down, that can bring us to the point of "withering away."

This isn't what God intends for us. We were not made to wither, to slink back because we're too tired and because the world won't notice if *we*, the moms, don't shine. We were made to thrive, to *flourish*.

What does this mean? What does this look like in the daily and often overwhelming demands of motherhood and busy lives? It looks like caring for ourselves as well as everyone around us. Of course, this is not new advice. We moms hear this a lot: "Take care of yourself!" When we hear it from magazines or mom bloggers, often they mean that we should sneak in a visit to the local spa for a refreshing mani-pedi. And that's not a bad treat. But it's not the long-term recipe for flourishing.

If we want to flourish rather than wither—even during the most difficult times of motherhood—taking care of ourselves must mean avoiding burnout by taking care of all of us. Our hearts, minds, bodies, and souls. We need to indulge not just in things that make us *look* good, but in things that make us *feel* good. We need to make time for the things of life that stretch us mentally and physically, that bring us closer to God, that involve our minds, that stir up our hearts. And if we want to flourish we need to find ways to build rest into our lives. This may not even come in the form of a much-needed nap or eight hours straight of sleep. But it must come in the choices we make for our days, in giving ourselves permission to say "no" to activities that drain us and to say "yes" to things that nourish us, so that we aren't always running ragged, on empty, and so that we can flourish for ourselves, for our kids, and for the kingdom of God.

Response

God, I'm tired. Worn out. I have a hard time building rest into my life and yet I know it's something you want for me. My need to rest is a reflection of you. Help me to find a rhythm of life that allows for all life's tasks and demands, but also for time to recover so that I can truly flourish and live as you've called me to.

What does God say? See Genesis 2:2–3.

You Are Made to Follow God

Psalm 81:13–14

If my people would only listen to me,
    if Israel would only follow my ways,
how quickly I would subdue their enemies
    and turn my hand against their foes!

When my son finally got up to get his shoes after the *third* time being told, I held his little face and asked, "Why can't you just obey me the first time I ask?"

He smiled and shrugged. "Because I was *busy*," he said.

I laughed, although it really wasn't funny. Sure, his disobedience this time wasn't of the live-or-die variety, but the broader point was how easily he had dismissed me. It took a raised volume and a greater sense of urgency in my voice to spur him to action.

Why is that so? Probably for the very reason he said: he was busy. Busy making a train track out of his sister's subtraction flash cards. You know how that goes.

While I ended up talking to him in the car ride to preschool about how he had to obey Mama when she told him to do something whether or not he was busy, it proved to be yet another moment in my life where I was convicted of my own hypocrisy mid-lecture.

I'm actually not one to rebel against rules—at least not the human-made sort. I wasn't speeding on the way to school. I follow recipes. I make deadlines. But when it comes to *God's* rules, I tend to get a little too busy to follow a few of them.

Like, honoring the Sabbath. Who has time to rest? Who has time for a whole day of *not* working? Not me!

Like, loving our neighbors. Sure, I'll say hi and everything. But I'm so busy with my own family and my work and my church, who can find time to sit with the lonely widow down the street? Not me!

But just as the rules we set for our kids are not arbitrary or made on a whim to complicate our kids' lives for no reason, God's rules for us are not willy-nilly instructions meant to complicate our lives further.

Just as we give our kids rules because we love them—and expect our rules to be followed because they are what makes family life run smoother and more lovingly—so God gives us rules because he loves us. God gives us rules because they make our lives *better*. Because when we follow God, we are living life the way it honors God, others, and ourselves.

We were *made* to follow God. It's the business of life—all the distractions and temptations—that keep us from walking in his steps, from following the guidelines he sets out for us and, ultimately, from living life as he intends for us to live it. We rob ourselves of a better life when we get too busy or too distracted to follow God.

Response

God, I know you don't give rules to burden us or to set unrealistic expectations but that you give us guidelines for the same reason I set rules for my kids: because you love us and because you want to see us live right. Help me to follow your commands and to live as you would have me live—because I love you.

What does God say? See Matthew 9:13.

You Are Made to Be Near God

Psalm 84:1–4

How lovely is your dwelling place,
  LORD Almighty!
My soul yearns, even faints,
  for the courts of the LORD;
my heart and my flesh cry out
  for the living God.
Even the sparrow has found a home,
  and the swallow a nest for herself,
  where she may have her young—
a place near your altar,
  LORD Almighty, my King and my God.
Blessed are those who dwell in your house;
  they are ever praising you.

While I readily admit that I love having time to myself, time away from the seemingly unrelenting demands of having my three kids around, I must also admit that never am I happier than when every member of my family is safe and sound. Right near me.

Especially on nights when the weather is turning, when snow or rainstorms are expected, nothing feels better than knowing that my babies, my husband, and even my dog are safe and sound within the warm and dry confines of our house.

I love having my family near. All seems right with the world when we are together. As if it's what we were made for. And, of course, we were! While certainly we all have our own places to be at different times of the day or week, family is made to be together, to be near.

My longing to have my family near reminds me of how God feels about us. Throughout Scripture, we see evidence of God's mourning and even anger over times when his children wandered away from him. In fact, in Matthew 23:37, Jesus says, "Jerusalem, Jerusalem . . . how often I have longed to gather your children together, as a hen gathers her chicks under her wings, and you were not willing."

God is like a mother hen—and a mother human! He wants his children near, in his courts, praising him, as today's psalm says. And if we're honest, we must realize it's what we want too.

But oftentimes—especially during times of doubt or confusion or frustration—we find it hard to be near God, to seek shelter in his wings. Sometimes, we just don't know how to be close when God seems so distant.

Drawing close to God, following those cries of our hearts to be near to him, is simply a matter of taking our hearts—our honest hearts—to him. When we feel distant or are filled with doubt, we should *tell* God that. Likewise, when we feel joyful or grateful, we should tell God that too. When we just don't know *what* to say, we can simply say, "God, I seek your presence. I long to be near." And then sit in silence before him, believing that he is with us, whether we feel it or not.

Just as we long for the company of our kids, so God longs for our company, our nearness.

Response

God, sometimes you feel so far away, and yet I long to have you near. Please come close to me, draw me to you, and let me know you are with me.

What does God say? See James 4:8.

You Are Made to Make Life Count

Psalm 39:4

> Show me, LORD, my life's end
> and the number of my days;
> let me know how fleeting my life is.

When my oldest son was probably three and my daughter one, I told a friend I thought motherhood was boring. I ended up writing the story—of how scary that was to say out loud, how ashamed I was of feeling that way—in my book *Mama's Got a Fake I.D.* and mentioning the story in a blog post.

Since then, I've been asked about this story what seems like a million times from readers, from radio interviewers, from other friends. So now this emotion I was so ashamed of sharing—but did anyway—gets brought up much more often than I'd like.

I'm still not proud of admitting that for a season my life as an at-home mom bored me. But having the story come up gives me an opportunity to dive a bit deeper into what I meant, to explore why exactly I felt bored for that time. Certainly, life was plenty busy—with raising two little kids, with squeezing in some freelance editing gigs, with volunteering at church, with trying to keep up a home and a relationship with my husband. Certainly there was a lot going on. So what could've made me feel bored?

As I look back on that time, I realize my boredom had little to do with the actual events or circumstances of my life and everything to do with my feeling *toward* them. Honestly, I had begun to believe the things that filled my life—even the important things like taking care of my babies every day—didn't matter all that much in the long run. Sure, I knew that being a mom was among the most important roles I could have, but still, the tedium of the tasks grated on me.

While my attitude about the *boringness* of my life wasn't great, it was born out of something natural, something built into us. We are made to want to make every day count. It's certainly how the psalmist felt—wanting to know how many days he had to live. In fact, it was during that tedious-seeming (or "boring") time of my life that I realized something: If I believed that being a mother mattered, if I believed being an editor or a writer mattered, if I believed that being a wife and a church member mattered, then even the little, tedious things—no matter how "boring"—about those roles mattered. At least to God. And so they should to me.

We are made to make life matter, to do things that glorify God and change this world. But we need to remember that what matters to God isn't usually what matters to the world. The small stuff, the big stuff, the boring stuff, and the exciting stuff all matter. When it's part of who we are, and when we do it to the glory of God.

Response

God, I hear stories of people doing "great" things and then look at my own life and wonder if what I'm doing day after day after day matters at all. I'm thankful for my life as a mom, for the gifts of my children, but sometimes struggle to find fulfillment in my days. Help me to see my life—and what I do—as you do. And help me to worship you in everything.

What does God say? See 1 Corinthians 10:31.

PART 7

You Are Given Fresh Starts

*For the director of music. A psalm of David.
When the prophet Nathan came to him after David
had committed adultery with Bathsheba.*

Have mercy on me, O God,
　　according to your unfailing love;
according to your great compassion
　　blot out my transgressions.
Wash away all my iniquity
　　and cleanse me from my sin.

For I know my transgressions,
　　and my sin is always before me.
Against you, you only, have I sinned
　　and done what is evil in your sight;
so you are right in your verdict
　　and justified when you judge.
Surely I was sinful at birth,
　　sinful from the time my mother conceived me.
Yet you desired faithfulness even in the womb;
　　you taught me wisdom in that secret place.

Cleanse me with hyssop, and I will be clean;
　　wash me, and I will be whiter than snow.

Let me hear joy and gladness;
    let the bones you have crushed rejoice.
Hide your face from my sins
    and blot out all my iniquity.

Create in me a pure heart, O God,
    and renew a steadfast spirit within me.
Do not cast me from your presence
    or take your Holy Spirit from me.
Restore to me the joy of your salvation
    and grant me a willing spirit, to sustain me.

Then I will teach transgressors your ways,
    so that sinners will turn back to you.
Deliver me from the guilt of bloodshed, O God,
    you who are God my Savior,
    and my tongue will sing of your righteousness.
Open my lips, LORD,
    and my mouth will declare your praise.
You do not delight in sacrifice, or I would bring it;
    you do not take pleasure in burnt offerings.
My sacrifice, O God, is a broken spirit;
    a broken and contrite heart
    you, God, will not despise.

May it please you to prosper Zion,
    to build up the walls of Jerusalem.
Then you will delight in the sacrifices of the righteous,
    in burnt offerings offered whole;
    then bulls will be offered on your altar.

Psalm 51

You Are Forgiven

Psalm 51:1–2, 10

Have mercy on me, O God,
  according to your unfailing love;
according to your great compassion
  blot out my transgressions.
Wash away all my iniquity
  and cleanse me from my sin. . . .
Create in me a pure heart, O God,
  and renew a steadfast spirit within me.

For someone as beloved by God as David was, he sure knew how to mess up. David's sins weren't just the "little" ones either. With David, we're not talking telling his grandmother he loved her cooking when in fact he thought it was too salty. We're talking the "big" stuff. David's sins were the sorts of sins that you would *think* might make God actually love him less.

In fact, when David penned these verses about needing God's mercy, about needing God to scrub away his sins, about needing a new, pure heart and a less-prone-to-stumble spirit, do you know what he had just done? Do you know the sins from which he was repenting?

David had just spied Bathsheba bathing. He had stared at her naked curves, water dripping off her limbs, and he had to have her. Literally. So, although David already had wives and concubines aplenty and although Bathsheba was married to another man, the Bible tells us, "David sent messengers to get her. She came to him, and he slept with her" (2 Sam. 11:4).

This sounds nicer than it was. This is the king "sending" for a woman. No romance. No mutuality. This is most likely sex against her will. This is horrible stuff. And it gets worse. Bathsheba ends up pregnant. Trouble is, her husband, Uriah, has been away at war. When David's plot to bring Uriah back home to sleep with Bathsheba so Uriah will assume paternity fails, David ends up sending Uriah back into war. To the front lines. To be killed.

You see what I mean about the big sins here? All in one story, we read of David's lust, his adultery, his violence, his deceit, and his murderous ways. No wonder he wants a clean heart. He needs one!

But truth be told, so do I. So do you. While we may not commit these "levels" of sins, we do sin. Every day. As moms we are probably more aware of our sins and our shortcomings than anyone on the planet—it's what fuels all that mommy guilt.

Realizing the depth and number of our sins is never fun. But here's the good news: God loves us so much he is ready and willing to forgive us of anything. Anything! Just as David went before God, asking for a new, clean heart and a "steadfast" spirit, so can we.

God loves us no matter what. And he stands ready to forgive us—to "blot out" our sins, as David writes here—no matter what. As moms we need to know this. Mothering out of a place where we know we are forgiven means we can live free of the guilt that weighs us down and then we can turn around and extend that loving grace to our kids.

Response

God, some days it's hard to believe you can love me no matter what. No matter what I do, think, or say, knowing that you love me still and stand ready to forgive me blows my mind. But I believe it. Thank you for this love that sent Jesus to stand in my place and to die for my sins.

What does God say? See John 3:16.

You Are Healed from Wounds

Psalm 51:17

My sacrifice, O God, is a broken spirit;
a broken and contrite heart
you, God, will not despise.

When my oldest son was two and I was seven months pregnant with my daughter, heartbreak entered my life—although I didn't recognize it as heartbreak when it first happened. After all, the term *broken heart* seems designated for the domain of love gone wrong. Not the life of the regular suburban at-home mom with a good marriage and a happy-enough family life.

But during an already difficult time when my parents separated and my husband's business took a couple of huge financial hits, our beloved dog died suddenly. My heart was left broken, something I finally recognized thanks to a quote from the introduction to James Herriot's *Favorite Dog Stories*. It read: "It is always said that however many wonderful and happy years a dog lives, you know that one day, the day he dies, your dog will break your heart."

Once I understood the pain of losing my dog was in fact brokenheartedness, it helped me recognize that pain as it manifested itself in different ways again and again during that time of my life.

I still don't look back on that period of my life with much *fond-ness*; I do look back at that period with much appreciation. Because I know my heart was broken then, I always recognize the ways God has healed my broken heart since then. While my life still shows some of the scars from those years, in so many ways, God has not only brought me through that pain, but he has healed me from it. Made me *better* for having lived through it, even!

I believe God did this for me because he loves me and because I eventually did what the psalmist suggests in today's verse: I offered God my broken heart. And God did not reject or "despise" it at all. It felt as though God held my heart in his hands and helped it heal.

Not one of us escapes having her heart broken. Sometimes it is love that breaks it, a relationship gone wrong. Sometimes it's because of death or tragedy. Sometimes it's something local, familiar that breaks our hearts. Other times, the break is caused by events or circumstances a world away.

Broken hearts always hurt, and we don't exactly *long* for them in our lives. And yet, when our hearts do break and when we do offer them as a "sacrifice" to God, the great Healer can perform miracles like we can hardly imagine.

God has used my broken heart to make me more into the woman and the mother he needed me to be. Having my heart break softened my heart—and I believe expanded it a bit. The newly healed heart *feels* much better than the old, unbroken model did.

When we hurt, when our hearts break, we need to do no more than offer them as gifts to God, asking him to heal us in his good time, but also to use our hurts—and our experience from healing—for the good.

Response

God, I'm hurting. My heart feels heavy and broken. I don't know what to do with my hurt sometimes. But I ask that you step in and heal these wounds. Help me in my recovery to not forget what it is to hurt so that I may use my pain for the good of others.

What does God say? See Genesis 50:20.

You Are Defined by God

Psalm 69:7–9

For I endure scorn for your sake,
    and shame covers my face.
I am a foreigner to my own family,
    a stranger to my own mother's children;
for zeal for your house consumes me,
    and the insults of those who insult you fall on me.

Before Psalm 69 begins, we see a little note that these words are to be sung to the tune of "Lilies." This makes me smile. Though it probably shouldn't. But I smile because although I have no idea what the tune "Lilies" sounds like, since a lily is a rather happy-looking flower and the sprouting of lilies is a happy event, I imagine that a song called "Lilies" would be up-tempo. A joyous little number to get you up off your bottom and moving a bit.

I imagine people smiling and clapping and laughing and tossing their heads back while "Lilies" is played.

But then there are the *words* of Psalm 69. This psalm is a lament if there ever was one. The words sink readers right into the lily pond that perhaps David was stuck in when he wrote this. David is enduring scorn and shame for following God. David's own family thought he was out of his mind for believing God with the passion that he did. I imagine that David's family called him "crazy," "foolish," maybe "stupid" for following God's call on his life the way he did. David made no sense to them.

Can you relate to this? I don't understand true persecution as we've seen it carried out through history and the way it continues to be carried out across the globe—with torturous suffering for loving Jesus. I do understand a bit about scorn, though.

My family—though they are believers—have at times thought I was a little off my rocker for taking a job with a low-paying, not-for-profit Christian publishing company instead of pursuing more lucrative "secular" options. My family questions our decision to forgo vacations and new cars to send our kids to a Christian school. My family wonders why I choose to tell some of the stories I do when I write. Don't they realize how I might embarrass myself (and them)?

Sometimes the choices we make as we seek to be the women God is calling us to be make no sense to our families, our friends, or our neighbors. And oftentimes, these people are all willing to tell us that it makes little or no sense!

These are the times when I find myself second-guessing—trying to figure out once again who I am, what I'm supposed to do. But it always comes back to this: We are defined by God. Not by anyone else. No matter how important those people are to us. What matters in life—what we do with our gifts and our time and our relationships—is that we're doing what God has called us to do. Even when it seems downright silly.

And although facing scorn from others is never fun, living the journey God has placed us on is fun—rewarding, blessed, filled with unexpected treasures. So maybe "Lilies" is indeed a happy tune. Because maybe David just knew that as difficult as life was for him in that moment, as difficult as it was facing scorn from those he loved, following God is always worth getting up and dancing about.

Response

God, people don't always respect the choices I make for my life or for my family. Some think I'm silly because I make decisions I believe honor you but that go against what our culture thinks we should do. Help me to ignore the voices of those who don't understand and help me to seek only your approval.

What does God say? See 1 Timothy 4:12–15.

You Are Redeemed

Psalm 103:2–5

> Praise the LORD, my soul,
>   and forget not all his benefits—
> who forgives all your sins
>   and heals all your diseases,
> who redeems your life from the pit
>   and crowns you with love and compassion,
> who satisfies your desires with good things
>   so that your youth is renewed like the eagle's.

"God doesn't waste anything so neither should we," my friend said as she dusted spilled Frosted Flakes off her table and back into the box.

While I agreed with her in sentiment, I said I might have given those bits to my dog. My friend's table, however, was also a lot cleaner than mine is on most days.

But she knew that with a brood of preschoolers in the house—each learning to pour their own cereal, to take care of their own needs bit by bit—there would be accidents. There would be spills. None of it—not the actual spilled material or the lesson itself—needed to be wasted.

Good advice. Especially since my friend is so right about God not wasting anything. We make lots of mistakes, spill lots of cereal on the table, if you will. And God wastes none of it. Doesn't even toss it to the dogs (well, maybe he does. I happen to believe that God loves dogs too).

Our God is a redeemer. He's not one to just let us wallow in our mishaps. Right from the first moment when Adam and Eve sinned, God got a plan going, a plan to redeem humankind from this disastrous mistake. And throughout each bit of human history—from the fall to Jesus to us today—God has been working in this world through his people to redeem it and to use even our mistakes for his glory.

How wonderful is that? It's so freeing to know that when we mess up—and we all mess up—not only are we forgiven, but God can also take our mistakes, even our deepest sins, and turn them around. This doesn't mean we won't face the consequences of our actions, but that God can use them for good. Perhaps to teach us, perhaps to give us greater empathy, perhaps to ignite a new passion. We never know how he will use our mistakes, how he will redeem our sins, but we do know that if we seek him and if we ask him to, he will.

Response

God, thank you for taking my mistakes and flipping them right around, for redeeming them, and for not letting them go to waste. Thank you for using every last thing in my life as an opportunity to learn more about you and how you might have me live. Thank you that I don't have to be afraid to make mistakes as I step out in faith because I know that you have called me by name and that you have redeemed me.

What does God say? See Isaiah 43:1.

You Are Given a Second Chance

Psalm 25:7

Do not remember the sins of my youth
and my rebellious ways;
according to your love remember me,
for you, LORD, are good.

I know I'm not the only one who looks forward to September
every year. Although I am a huge fan of the laziness and warmth
and late-nights-on-the-porch and splashing-in-the-lake-ness of
summertime, every year by August, I start to itch for September.

Not just because my kids are starting to grate on each other's
nerves and I'm eager for some much needed alone-in-my-own-
home time. Those of us who long for September, for the change
in leaves and that cool smell in the wind, are really longing for
the fresh start September offers. Most of us spent enough time
having September through June mark our years that the back-
to-school season still means starting anew, even more than the
actual New Year.

Even if we returned to a school we attended the year before,
each new year, each new grade, each new class meant a second
chance. That second chance to do maybe a little better on tests,

to read more, to practice more, to make that team this time, to make that better friend.

During the newness of a new school year we understand fresh starts and second chances are among the great luxuries of life. And they are luxuries God offers us every day—or every time we turn to him.

The beautiful thing about a life spent with God—following him, loving him, being loved *by* him—is that his grace through Jesus Christ offers us opportunities to have our slates wiped clean. Although we may still face the consequences of mistakes or sins committed in our lives, when we ask Jesus to forgive us, those sins are gone. Wiped from our slates. Erased from our permanent records. God no longer sees them. And we don't have to focus on them either.

It's easy to get bogged down in remembering ways we've messed up—especially when we become moms. Many of us revisit the mistakes we made even long before we had kids, feel the guilt of sins committed before we knew better. There's something about the responsibility of motherhood—the stress of it, probably—that calls to light the ways we've messed up, that brings to mind the "sins of our youth" and our "rebellious ways," as the psalmist calls them.

But God doesn't want us to bring those sins to mind every day. He doesn't want us to raise our kids with our eyes focused on the mistakes of our past. If we follow God and have sought his forgiveness through Jesus Christ, God wants us to live into the second chance that he gives us every time we seek his grace. He wants us to live secure in the knowledge that our sins were erased from his view of us when Jesus Christ died on the cross for our sins. When we ask for forgiveness, God doesn't look at us and see our sin anymore. He sees his beloved children. And that's a great place to mother from—as women who sin, but women God loves enough to always give another chance, a fresh start.

Response

God, thank you for fresh starts and second chances. Thank you for new mercies that meet me every day. And just as I live in the luxury of your grace, help me extend that grace to those around me.

What does God say? See Lamentations 3:22–23.

PART 8

You Are Worthy

A psalm.

Sing to the LORD a new song,
for he has done marvelous things;
his right hand and his holy arm
have worked salvation for him.
The LORD has made his salvation known
and revealed his righteousness to the nations.
He has remembered his love
and his faithfulness to Israel;
all the ends of the earth have seen
the salvation of our God.

Shout for joy to the LORD, all the earth,
burst into jubilant song with music;
make music to the LORD with the harp,
with the harp and the sound of singing,
with trumpets and the blast of the ram's horn—
shout for joy before the LORD, the King.

Let the sea resound, and everything in it,
the world, and all who live in it.
Let the rivers clap their hands,
let the mountains sing together for joy;

let them sing before the LORD,
    for he comes to judge the earth.
He will judge the world in righteousness
    and the peoples with equity.

Psalm 98

You Are Worthy of Being Known

Psalm 11:4

> The LORD is in his holy temple;
>   the LORD is on his heavenly throne.
> He observes everyone on earth;
>   his eyes examine them.

I've loved the story of "Zacchaeus the Tax Collector" since I was little. It's a favorite for so many reasons. I love that Zacchaeus climbed a sycamore-fig tree. I imagine him munching on a fig while craning around, looking for Jesus. And I love, love, love the moment when Jesus spots Zacchaeus, calls his name, and invites himself over to his house for dinner.

The moment is classic Jesus. In one sentence he manages to horrify those around him (dinner with a tax collector?) and totally change the trajectory of one man's life. And I love Jesus for this act for a couple of reasons. First, because in inviting himself to Zacchaeus's house for dinner, Jesus once again declared that his message, his love, his grace, his healing power, his *everything* extended to even the "worst" of sinners, the most hated and despised—and in those days you couldn't do much worse than collecting taxes. But beyond that, I love Jesus for this because in inviting himself over for dinner—which would involve hours of lounging and eating and chatting—Jesus declared in front of a parade of startled witnesses that Zacchaeus was worth knowing.

Zacchaeus wasn't simply a stereotypical villain everyone else brushed off. He was a complex man—sinful, to be sure, but beloved by God and worth getting to know.

Once upon a time I felt trapped behind the "mom stereotype," a time when I felt nobody really got to know me because, after all, I was a mom. *Everybody* knows what a mom is, right? According to many, we all vote the same, think the same, buy the same brand of peanut butter—if we're "choosy," that is.

In our world where we love to slap on labels and make quick judgments about everyone, and yet feel so lonely when it's done to us, I find it so refreshing that Jesus doesn't see people the way the world sees people. God never looks at us as stereotypes or caricatures. When God "observes everyone on earth" and when "his eyes examine them," as today's psalm says, God sees us as individual people—each of us with different personalities, interests, passions, ideas, loves, feelings, dreams, desires. God sees us as women worth having dinner with, worth getting to know.

Response

God, thank you for knowing me inside and out. Thank you for appreciating my quirks and for helping to refine my faults. Thank you for taking the time to get to know me as the woman I am.

What does God say? See Psalm 139:1–3.

You Are Worthy of Being Loved

Psalm 98:3

He has remembered his love
and his faithfulness to Israel;
all the ends of the earth have seen
the salvation of our God.

Her words came quick—like she'd had them ready and waiting in her mind for years before she had the guts to utter them: "I think I'm unlovable."

I tried to assure her it wasn't true; I reminded her how much her kids loved her. But she pressed on, clarified. Yes, Kay knew that her children loved her. She knew her friends loved or at least cared about her, but when it came to men who loved her enough to stick around or parents who loved her enough to offer support, she'd finally accepted that it wasn't meant to be in her life. She concluded she was unlovable.

I never saw Kay again after our conversation. She, like many people, had confided in me after I spoke to her MOPS group. Sometimes it's safer to share our painful secrets with strangers than with friends. But her words still haunt me. Kay believed them so deeply. And I know she's not the only one who's felt that way.

Motherhood—once we've experienced the depth of love we feel for our own kids—can cause us to wonder about the love we have or haven't felt toward ourselves. The blessed among us appreciate the depth of love our parents had for us. Others of us cling to the love of our husbands. But some of us are hit with the realization that we've never really known the kind of love we've wanted. Or that we've never really been loved at all. For still others, it's that we've known love—but lost it.

No matter what our experience with love has been, surely each of us can relate a bit to Kay. Each of us has wondered at times whether we really are worthy of love.

If we base the answer to that question on human love, even those of us who've felt true, real, deep love in our lives may be left wondering. But if we base the answer to that question on God's view of us, we never have to think twice.

God loves us. He always has. Always will. And if God—the King of the universe, the Lord of Creation, our Savior and Redeemer—loves us? Then we are worthy. Worthy of love, of being loved.

Response

God, sometimes I feel so unlovable, so unworthy of anyone's love, let alone yours. But then I think of how I love my kids—how I love them no matter how they act up or act out—and I understand how you love me. Thank you for loving me even when I am unlovable. Thank you for declaring me worthy of your astonishing love and mercy.

What does God say? See Zephaniah 3:17.

You Are Worthy of Respect

Psalm 78:1–4

My people, hear my teaching;
    listen to the words of my mouth.
I will open my mouth with a parable;
    I will utter hidden things, things from of old—
things we have heard and known,
    things our ancestors have told us.
We will not hide them from their descendants;
    we will tell the next generation
the praiseworthy deeds of the Lord,
    his power, and the wonders he has done.

During a recent political campaign, one local candidate accused another of being a misogynist. Twenty or so years earlier, the candidate had said, "We don't need any housewives in the General Assembly."

We mothers—whether or not we'd classify ourselves as "housewives"—tend not to get the biggest heapings of respect. It's not that people don't value the work of moms—they do! And it's not that people don't love mothers—they do!

But when it comes to, say, issues involving the brain, when people think of us first and foremost as mothers, most assume our brains are not up to the task. Which is why, I'd guess, this politician made this horrible comment about not wanting housewives serving the state of Illinois. Our brains are mush. You know, unlike lawyer or politician minds.

While we all know it isn't true (because our minds still do work wonderfully) that being a mom doesn't make us dumb or incapable of grappling with the issues of the world, the truth is this: the more we hear words that minimize a mother's contributions, the more these sentiments are inferred, the less we feel the respect we deserve. Not as brainiacs, not even as mothers. But as human beings.

Each of us—no matter where we are or what we do—is worthy of respect. Not because of anything we have done, but because of what God did when he created each of us. He gave every single one of us dignity—dignity that soaks deep into our gifts and talents, into our personalities, into every unique fiber of our being that makes us . . . *us*.

So while the world may sometimes look down on us and our "mommy brains," remember that God does no such thing. The psalmist knew this when he wrote, "My people, hear my teaching; listen to the words of my mouth. I will open my mouth with a parable; I will utter hidden things."

We all have "hidden things" that God gave us to share with the world—whether through words or deeds. We all have a special something to bring to this planet, something that leaves a mark God wanted there. God is waiting for us to leave these marks. What are *you* waiting for?

Response

God, while I'm not hoping for undue admiration, I'm so tired of the people who look down on me for being a mom, who think less of me—and my mind—because I have children. Help me to ignore hurtful remarks and to live into the truth that no matter how the world sees me or my role, you love and treasure me.

What does God say? See Proverbs 31.

You Are Worthy
of Maintaining Boundaries

Psalm 74:15–17

It was you who opened up springs and streams;
    you dried up the ever-flowing rivers.
The day is yours, and yours also the night;
    you established the sun and moon.
It was you who set all the boundaries of the earth;
    you made both summer and winter.

My life as a work-from-home mom feels blessed on most days. I'm aware of the privilege I enjoy being able to do some of the things I love professionally —write and edit and speak and encourage—based out of the place where I get to do another thing I love personally—raise my kids.

But this arrangement has one huge challenge: my life often feels boundary-less. Each part of my life—the paid parts, the volunteer parts, the mama parts, the wife parts—runs into the others. They all swirl and mingle. *Sometimes* this leaves a beautiful and wondrous design. But oftentimes—okay, *most* times—the swirls and mingles of my life resemble more of a disastrous spill. A huge mess.

Without any defined space and time and boundaries, my life can get confusing and stressful. For everyone in it. Although I recognized this problem early on in my life as a mom-wife-writer-speaker-editor, honestly, I thought I should be so blessed that I was able to have each of these roles as part of my life, that I was able to do this with only minimal childcare, that I began to believe that I didn't deserve to lay down any laws, to create any boundaries.

How wrong I was.

Right from the get-go in the Bible—right in the story of creation—we see God establishing boundaries. He created night and day, earth and sky, water and land, fish and birds, men and women. And he created six days to work and one to rest. In fact, with the creation of the Sabbath—a day of rest—we see that even God has boundaries. He carved out a time to rest—a boundary in his infinite life.

The psalmist tells us that God is "who set all the boundaries of the earth" and cites the creation of seasons as an example of this. If God created this earth to have boundaries, then that means our *lives* were created to have boundaries too. Just as we lay down rules for our families and our kids as boundaries, so should we set up rules and boundaries for ourselves.

We need boundaries—perhaps boundaries for "me" time, for work time, for God time, for hobby time, for exercise time. God created us this way. Just as fences take some work to put up in a yard, so will personal boundaries require some work. Perhaps it's finding creative babysitting options. Perhaps it's discipline techniques to reinforce boundaries, or perhaps it's simply figuring out that one special DVD you can pop in that engrosses your kids and gives you a boundary. Definitely it means the hard work of learning to say "no"—to our kids, to our churches, to our work, to our extended family—whenever they attempt to cross a boundary.

Living with boundaries doesn't always feel easy. But it always feels worth it. God *gave* us boundaries, and we are worthy of using them.

Response

*God, I'm grateful for the many "hats" I wear in my life.
I'm thankful that you have put me in a position to be many
things to many people and to use my talents in a variety of
ways. But, God, sometimes I have trouble saying "no" and
maintaining good boundaries. Please help me draw lines—
lines to protect time for myself, for my family, and for you.*

What does God say? See Mark 1:35; 14:32–34.

You Are Worthy of Being Still

Psalm 46:10

Be still, and know that I am God;
   I will be exalted among the nations,
   I will be exalted in the earth.

"Mama, can you help me find my shoes?"

"Did you check your room?"

"Can *you* check my room? You're just sitting there doing nothing."

And so went the conversation between my son Henrik and me before the family left for church last Sunday. Henrik was right. I *was* sitting on the sofa doing nothing. It wasn't because he was wrong that I got mad. It was the implication that it was better for *me* to scurry around the house and look for the shoes Henrik had taken off and not put away so that *Henrik* could sit on the sofa and do nothing.

Henrik is ten—so although I made him keep looking for his shoes, I can't fault him too much for his thinking. To a child, a mom's role is to *help* them, right? I believe that's good—and fair. I'm almost always glad to help my kids—to rush to their aid, to lend a hand, to do whatever. But I'm always trying to instill in my kids that while I am mostly happy to help them, I am not the help. I'm not their personal servant—waiting for them to clap their hands and order me off to the next desire I can fulfill of theirs. And I try to teach them that Mama needs times to sit and do nothing.

In the midst of my run-around, nonstop life, I need time to be still. So do you. We need it physically, emotionally, and spiritually. Our bodies, minds, and souls all need to be stilled every now and again. All at the same time! And yet, how often we forget this. Even if we let ourselves *sit* for a minute during the day, often our brains and souls keep running.

The idea of being still goes beyond simply sitting. Stillness isn't about kicking back on the sofa and clicking on the TV or clicking over to Facebook. To "be still and know that I am God" as we read in today's psalm speaks more of a disconnect, in a way, from what is around us. Even if only for a couple of moments.

Stillness is time to be. And that is it. To learn to be still means we learn to relax our bodies, calm our minds, and open our souls—not to the usual worries or frets that push their way in, but to the Holy Spirit.

Being still and knowing that God is God isn't written as a suggestion. It's a command. Not because God wants to boss us around, but because he loves us enough to declare us *worthy* of getting to know the Almighty. Therefore, we are worthy of time to be still—and to get to know God. Whether or not kids need help finding their shoes.

Response

God, I feel life rushing around me. I long for peace but can't seem to find it. Help me be still. Calm me. So that I may know you better.

What does God say? See Psalm 23.

PART 9

You Are Loved by God

A psalm of David.

The LORD is my shepherd, I lack nothing.
　　He makes me lie down in green pastures,
he leads me beside quiet waters,
　　he refreshes my soul.
He guides me along the right paths
　　for his name's sake.
Even though I walk
　　through the darkest valley,
I will fear no evil,
　　for you are with me;
your rod and your staff,
　　they comfort me.

You prepare a table before me
　　in the presence of my enemies.
You anoint my head with oil;
　　my cup overflows.
Surely your goodness and love will follow me
　　all the days of my life,
and I will dwell in the house of the LORD
　　forever.

Psalm 23

You Are the Apple of God's Eye

Psalm 17:7–8

> Show me the wonders of your great love,
>   you who save by your right hand
>   those who take refuge in you from their foes.
> Keep me as the apple of your eye;
>   hide me in the shadow of your wings.

Through David's words in the psalms, we read of his love, his anger, his fears, his praises, his insecurities, and his arrogance all being brought before God. It is, as Donald Miller has called it, a "fearless"* approach. Especially considering that many of us think we need to speak to God in a formal, stilted manner. Or that we need to *hide* what we really feel or think from God. As if he cannot see what's in our minds and in our hearts.

I wonder if it was this fearlessness in bringing his love and anger and everything else before God that made David so special to and so beloved by God. In today's psalm David refers to himself as the apple of God's eye—a term we now know to mean someone of great affection, someone we dote upon, someone for whom we'd do anything.

* March 14, 2012, Donald Miller's author/fan page on Facebook.

Of course, David isn't the only apple of God's eye. We see it used in other places in Scripture, about other people. In Zechariah 2:8, God speaks to all of Israel when he says, "For whoever touches you touches the apple of his eye."

God's people are the apples of his eye. This is good news for you and me! Through the grace and love of Jesus Christ, we can claim this honor too. And that's astonishing to consider, really. The Lord of all creation looks at you and looks at me and sees us as his apples, as people whom he loves, upon whom he dotes, for whom he'd do anything.

You are the apple of God's eye. He loves you. He dotes on you. He'd do anything for you. Think about what this means: No matter what you feel, no matter what you think, no matter whether you're joyful or disappointed, whether you're confident or terrified, whether you're good with life or feeling a bit spent, take it to God. He dotes on you; he'd do anything for you. Through Jesus Christ's sacrifice on the cross, he's done *everything* for you, the apple of his eye.

Response

God, what a thrill it is to imagine you never losing sight of me. How wonderful it is to go through life knowing there is not a place I can go, not a thing I can do that you will not see, that you will not keep a loving, watchful eye on. Thank you for the kind of love that keeps me as the apple of your eye.

What does God say? See 1 John 3:1.

You Are Favored

Psalm 30:5

For his anger lasts only a moment,
　　but his favor lasts a lifetime;
weeping may stay for the night,
　　but rejoicing comes in the morning.

A colleague recently shared some exciting news. "After a long time of God saying 'no,'" she wrote, "God just said 'yes.'" And then she revealed what God apparently had in store for her and her family.

Her words could not have come at a better time for me. I was smack-dab in the middle of a time when God seemed to be all about "no" when it came to my requests. My family seemed stalled in that horrible waiting season—sometimes even going down into the "depths" David speaks about in Psalm 30:1. I wondered if we'd done something or if we were being punished by God, and maybe that was why he seemed to be leaving us hanging.

But my friend's perspective—adding later in her email that she believed God had said "no" to leave room for the big "yes" to this opportunity—echoed something that is seen throughout Scripture and throughout the lives of the faithful. God often says "no" and we assume the worst; we have a hard time believing God still has good in mind for us.

Even David felt this way. He writes in Psalm 30:6–7, "When I felt secure, I said, 'I will never be shaken.' LORD, when you favored me, you made my royal mountain stand firm; but when you hid your face, I was dismayed."

David felt this way for the same reason we all do: because we don't know. We don't ever really know what God is up to. We often don't and can't understand "his ways," as we like to say. So when we are faced with the "no" from God, we too feel dismayed. We wonder why God is not stepping in.

And yet, David understood that even when it seems God is angry and withholding his hand from us for a time, it doesn't last. Even when we have the roughest nights with God, we find ourselves rejoicing in the morning. David knew this from his experience with God—from realizing that he was favored.

Just like David, we are favored by God. While we think of being "favored" as being preferred to everyone else, this, of course, doesn't mean that God loves us *better* than he loves others, but that he favors—or chooses—us for certain things (David was favored for king of Israel; you were favored to be mom to your kids) and that he *bestows* his favor on us.

And I love to think of what God's bestowing of favors looks like. A favor, of course, can mean a kind act or a token of love or appreciation. Or favor can mean approval. How wonderful to know that God favors us—that he approves of us, that he does kind acts toward us, that he offers us tokens of his love.

We are favored by God. All the time. Even when it feels as though God has turned away from us—and filled our lives with "nos"— God favors us. My friend learned that even God's "no" for many years of her life was a sign of his favor—a gift. Because in all those nos, God was either sparing or preparing them. And always keeping them in his favor.

Response

God, help me to recognize your "favor" toward me—no matter what form it takes. And help me to believe deep in my core that you always have the best in mind for me—even when your answers are not what I want.

What does God say? See Luke 11:11.

You Are Sought and Welcomed

Psalm 23:6

> Surely your goodness and love will follow me
> all the days of my life,
> and I will dwell in the house of the LORD forever.

"It's right there."

"Where?"

"There. Turn around."

How many times have you had a conversation like that with your kids? I'd guess that we run through this—or a variation of it—every day in our house (especially if I include my husband and his "Have you seen my keys?" conversation!). But with my kids I can guarantee that, at the very least, we run through this each morning as we get ready for school.

"Your homework? Right next to you."

"Your shoes? On the floor in front of you."

"Your lunch? In your backpack."

"Honey, you just gotta look."

I think of these conversations when I read today's famous words from the 23rd psalm: "Surely your goodness and love will *follow* me all the days of my life" (emphasis mine). I imagine David walking along, through the very places he shows us in this psalm—the "green pastures," the "quiet waters," the "right paths," the "darkest valley," and that banquet table before his enemies. And in each spot—whether the beautiful pasture or the terrifying valley—I imagine him turning and seeing the goodness and love of God, right with him, just a step behind him. "Surely," David wrote. He was sure that God's favor followed him every last day. No matter where he went. No matter what he had to do.

That's fantastic.

Especially during times when it's difficult to feel God's goodness or when we're unsure of God's love, I love that David opens up a wonderful—and truthful—reality. No matter where we are or must go, no matter what we have to do, God's love and goodness follow us. They are right there with us. What a comfort!

Of course, David was able to declare this with certainty because he stopped to turn around and look. He took the time to notice God. We need to do the same.

So often we become wrapped up in the minute preparations and the stress of what's coming that we fail to look around, fail to see what's right in front of or behind us or right next to us.

David's words are a lovely reminder to do what he did. Whether we're walking through the happiest places and times in life or we're traversing some rough and frightening terrain, when we seek God's goodness and love, we will find it. Because he's already seeking us. He's following us, waiting for us to turn and notice him. Every day. Every place.

Response

God, thank you for setting signs of your goodness and faithfulness all over this world and all through my life. Please help me notice you everywhere—and worshipfully respond to your presence.

What does God say? See Matthew 7:7.

You Are Chosen

Psalm 65:4

Blessed are those you choose
   and bring near to live in your courts!
We are filled with the good things of your house,
   of your holy temple.

My former boss used to tell a story (over and over and over again) about his response to school-yard bullies who teased him about being adopted. When the taunting would start, he'd point a finger and say, "Well, at least I know my parents *wanted* me. I was chosen."

While I'm not sure I'd recommend this as a response, I have to admit, each time I heard him tell this story, I smiled—sincerely. Because what he said was exactly true. While the bullies tried to torment him with the fact that someone gave him up, my boss clung to a greater truth: someone had chosen him.

There's nothing like being chosen. Just ask anyone who's ever been left out, left hanging on the sidelines of life, who's never been chosen, included, or asked. We've all experienced this on some level. Certainly in childhood, although we don't escape it in adulthood.

So here's what's so great about God: he chooses us. You are chosen. In sending his Son Jesus to die on the cross, paying the price for our sin, God pointed his finger at you, at me, at our families, and at our friends and said, essentially, "I choose you. To be on my team. To be a part of my family. To live with me, forever." Of course, it's up to us whether or not to accept his offer, his gift. But we can never say it isn't because God didn't want us. He does.

With all the rejection that comes with life—whether it's judgment we receive for our mothering or family choices, whether it's criticism we receive in our jobs or volunteering, whether it's that feeling of never really fitting in or belonging—it's such great comfort to know that God loves us enough to choose us to be his, forever. With God, we don't ever have to guess whether we're really wanted, whether we really belong. No matter what we do, we belong with God—because of what he's already done for us.

And beyond that, the psalmist says we are "blessed" in being chosen, that we are filled with the "good things" of God. Because when God chooses us, he doesn't simply let us hang. He's chosen us to be with him but also to do his will on earth—and in that he lavishes us with his love and blessings. I don't think this means he showers us with money or fame or those sorts of earthly understandings of "blessings." But, instead, it's when we live out who he's created (chosen) us to be here on earth, when we live who we are, that we find blessing in being chosen. In being able to live and experience love as God's chosen ones.

Response

God, I don't walk around saying, "God chose me!" but maybe I should—because it's a dazzling truth. Thank you for choosing me to be mom to my kids, for equipping me with gifts and talents to make a difference in this world, and for calling me your own.

What does God say? See 1 Peter 2:9.

135

You Are Provided For

Psalm 104:10–15

He makes springs pour water into the ravines;
    it flows between the mountains.
They give water to all the beasts of the field;
    the wild donkeys quench their thirst.
The birds of the sky nest by the waters;
    they sing among the branches.
He waters the mountains from his upper chambers;
    the land is satisfied by the fruit of his work.
He makes grass grow for the cattle,
    and plants for people to cultivate—
    bringing forth food from the earth:
wine that gladdens human hearts,
    oil to make their faces shine,
    and bread that sustains their hearts.

Once upon a time when I got to the "Give us today our daily bread" part of the Lord's Prayer, I'd have to wonder, think hard, what it might mean to rely on God literally for our daily bread.

While I have yet to experience true need in global or historic terms, in the past few years, my family has experienced enough financial stress to help me really understand what it means to depend on God. And God's been good.

I'd love to say that our debt was miraculously erased and all our bills are more than abundantly covered and that we've built our savings back up because of God's abundance toward us, but I can't. Instead, I can claim something better: experiencing God's daily provision and learning to trust and know him in a way I never could've imagined had we not struggled financially.

I believe Jesus taught us to pray for daily bread because it forces us to recognize that God is our provider and because it reminds us that we are not to worry about what we'll have three days, weeks, months, or years from now. Praying for our daily bread tells us that we are to be concerned about what we need for today—and we are to be trusting that God will provide.

Of course, you don't have to struggle financially to see this. "Daily bread" doesn't need to be literal bread. I've never actually longed for that yeasty mix of wheat and warm water when I've prayed this prayer. Our daily bread comes in many forms. Daily bread can be whatever we need to make it through that day.

Perhaps your daily bread is financial. Maybe it's wisdom that you need. Perhaps your daily bread is patience or mercy or love or pain relief. It could be almost anything. When we pray for our daily bread, we remember that God is *Jehovah Jireh*—our provider—and we recognize that all good and necessary things come from him. And just as he is the One who supplies all of creation with their needs, so he is the One who provides our needs.

Response

God, thank you for the ways you provide—financially, emotionally, and physically—for my family. Thank you for being a God who meets our needs and who carries our burdens. Help me recognize that your means of provision are not always what I would choose but that they are always the right way.

What does God say? See Matthew 6:25–34.

You Are Bestowed Upon

Psalm 84:11

> For the LORD God is a sun and shield;
> the LORD bestows favor and honor;
> no good thing does he withhold
> from those whose walk is blameless.

Some images of God just knock my socks off. Today's verse offers one of them. "For the LORD God is a sun and shield," the psalmist tells us. And I'm so glad he is. As someone whose idea of heaven is stretching out on a chaise lounge pool- or beach-side with a good book and a cool drink, soaking in the rays of the sun, the idea of God as sun works for me!

Of course, the days of me simply lying in the sun without worry are long gone. If I am poolside, I'm also eagle-eying my kids, making sure they stay safe, and if I am stretched under the sun, I'm also under plenty of SPF, a pair of sunglasses, and probably a big hat.

But it's not too difficult for me to put aside any potential dangers that now lurk even in sunbathing and imagine all the goodness the sun offers. Without sun, we have no light. Without sun, it's hard to get enough Vitamin D. Without sun, we have no warmth. Without sun, we have no life.

The sun bestows upon us all sorts of goodness—more than I can list here, more than I even know. And it bestows it upon *everyone*. The sun's goodness isn't simply for the lucky few, but for everyone under it.

While God gives us more than the sun ever could (especially since he gave us the sun itself!), as we try to understand God, we could do a lot worse than understand him as sun. Just as all we need to do to enjoy what the sun has to offer is to step out into it, so it is with God. God stands ready to bless us, to bestow all that he has upon us. He's already there, waiting to warm us with his love, to illuminate our lives with his grace, to nourish us with his very goodness.

On some days, in the harder times of life, when the clouds threaten to make us forget there ever was such a thing as sunshine, that God bestows his love and goodness on us can be hard to believe. But it's true nevertheless. We only need to step out into the goodness of God to feel what he offers.

Response

God, it's easy to forget all the ways you bless me. It's easy to get so caught up in my own life and the things I do under my own "steam" that I take for granted all you do and all you provide. Thank you for your abundant love and goodness. Thank you for bestowing upon me more blessings than I could ever count. Thank you, thank you, thank you for it all.

What does God say? See Matthew 5:45.

PART 10

You Are Called and Equipped

Of David.

Do not fret because of those who are evil
　　or be envious of those who do wrong;
for like the grass they will soon wither,
　　like green plants they will soon die away.

Trust in the LORD and do good;
　　dwell in the land and enjoy safe pasture.
Take delight in the LORD
　　and he will give you the desires of your heart.

Commit your way to the LORD;
　　trust in him and he will do this:
He will make your righteous reward shine like the dawn,
　　your vindication like the noonday sun.

Be still before the LORD
　　and wait patiently for him;
do not fret when people succeed in their ways,
　　when they carry out their wicked schemes.

Refrain from anger and turn from wrath;
　　do not fret—it leads only to evil.

For those who are evil will be destroyed,
  but those who hope in the LORD will inherit the land.

A little while, and the wicked will be no more;
  though you look for them, they will not be found.
But the meek will inherit the land
  and enjoy peace and prosperity.

The wicked plot against the righteous
  and gnash their teeth at them;
but the LORD laughs at the wicked,
  for he knows their day is coming.

The wicked draw the sword
  and bend the bow
to bring down the poor and needy,
  to slay those whose ways are upright.
But their swords will pierce their own hearts,
  and their bows will be broken.

Better the little that the righteous have
  than the wealth of many wicked;
for the power of the wicked will be broken,
  but the LORD upholds the righteous.

The blameless spend their days under the LORD's care,
  and their inheritance will endure forever.
In times of disaster they will not wither;
  in days of famine they will enjoy plenty.

But the wicked will perish:
  Though the LORD's enemies are like the flowers of the
  field,
  they will be consumed, they will go up in smoke.

The wicked borrow and do not repay,
  but the righteous give generously;

those the LORD blesses will inherit the land,
   but those he curses will be destroyed.

The LORD makes firm the steps
   of the one who delights in him;
though he may stumble, he will not fall,
   for the LORD upholds him with his hand.

I was young and now I am old,
   yet I have never seen the righteous forsaken
   or their children begging bread.
They are always generous and lend freely;
   their children will be a blessing.

Turn from evil and do good;
   then you will dwell in the land forever.
For the LORD loves the just
   and will not forsake his faithful ones.

Wrongdoers will be completely destroyed;
   the offspring of the wicked will perish.
The righteous will inherit the land
   and dwell in it forever.

The mouths of the righteous utter wisdom,
   and their tongues speak what is just.
The law of their God is in their hearts;
   their feet do not slip.

The wicked lie in wait for the righteous,
   intent on putting them to death;
but the LORD will not leave them in the power of the
   wicked
   or let them be condemned when brought to trial.

Hope in the LORD
   and keep his way.

He will exalt you to inherit the land;
  when the wicked are destroyed, you will see it.

I have seen a wicked and ruthless man
  flourishing like a luxuriant native tree,
but he soon passed away and was no more;
  though I looked for him, he could not be found.

Consider the blameless, observe the upright;
  a future awaits those who seek peace.
But all sinners will be destroyed;
  there will be no future for the wicked.

The salvation of the righteous comes from the LORD;
  he is their stronghold in time of trouble.
The LORD helps them and delivers them;
  he delivers them from the wicked and saves them,
  because they take refuge in him.

Psalm 37

You Are Mighty

Psalm 127:3–4

Children are a heritage from the LORD,
offspring a reward from him.
Like arrows in the hands of a warrior
are children born in one's youth.

When I was in college, a therapist asked me, "If you could pick any animal to describe yourself, what would it be?"

In my mind, I laughed at the cliché of this question. If you'd have asked me to guess what she'd ask—on this, my first visit with her—I'd have thrown this question on the list.

What kind of animal? What a stupid question.

But I thought about it anyway. Thought back to the reason I sat in her office. I thought of my parents, their marriage crumbling, again—while I was three hundred miles away. Where I couldn't "help." Where I couldn't protect my family.

"A grizzly bear," I said.

She smiled. I'm sure it seemed odd, the skinny, wimpy blonde student sitting across from her, thinking she was a grizzly. And then she asked why.

"Because they like fish and berries," I said. "And so do I. And because . . . I want to lash out at anyone or anything that tries to hurt my family. A mama grizzly, I guess."

I remembered this conversation ten years later, the evening my husband and I drove away from the hospital, me tucked in the backseat next to our two-day-old son. Suddenly, every other driver on the road now seemed like a public menace; everyone stopped next to us at stoplights seemed a potential threat to my baby.

Mama grizzly was back. With a vengeance.

While I *have* been a fighter, a defender my whole life (not a physical one, mind you. I really am quite wimpy), someone who's willing to jump into a fight that needs fighting, it had all been small potatoes before I had kids.

Once I had a baby—whose very life depended on me and my protection—everything ramped right up. Within me grew a fierceness, a might, that I could never have before imagined.

The strange thing was, this fierce and mighty protection instinct wasn't only for my own kids, but for *all* kids. For kids I had never met—and would never meet. For their moms. For their dads. Once I became a mom, the world seemed in so much greater need of defending, protecting.

It was odd. But I know it was God at work. I think we see that in Psalm 127:3–4. While many use this verse as the reason to have "quivers full" of children, I read it differently because it says children are *like* arrows.

While kids certainly aren't weapons (something I actually try to *remind* my kids of every now and again!), just *like* arrows make warriors mighty, strengthening and empowering them, our kids do that for us. Our love for them—our desire to protect them, to do right by them—fuels us to fight on their behalf.

Like having an arrow, having a child makes us fiercer. Sounds kind of horrible, but I believe it's the way God wants it. There are needs in this world that mothers, with our fierce, protective love, are uniquely equipped to meet.

This instinct to protect, to be mighty, is part of who we were called to be. It's one way we bear God's image. We were made to fight—for those we love and for those around us and for what is right. Kids give us great reason to do this.

Response

God, some days I feel so weak when the demands of life and of motherhood get to be too much. Fill me with your strength, with your might. On those days when my energy is low, let me tap into your amazing, sustaining power.

What does God say? See Ephesians 6:10.

You Are Called to the Unimagined

Psalm 78:70–73

He chose David his servant
and took him from the sheep pens;
from tending the sheep he brought him
to be the shepherd of his people Jacob,
of Israel his inheritance.
And David shepherded them with integrity of heart;
with skillful hands he led them.

My husband loves politics. I am not quite as big a fan, but because I love my husband, I follow local, statewide, and national races quite closely. Which means I realize how much all the candidates—no matter which party they are from, no matter which office they seek—tend to sound alike. Politicians tend to be clichés of themselves.

Consider any political mailing: often the candidates are sitting at a kitchen dinette with older folks to show how they listen, how they care. Often you'll see them standing in a warehouse, in a hard hat, perhaps holding a set of blueprints (they've got a plan!), or pointing to something off in the distance. The rapt gazes of the warehouse workers follow the pointed finger (they are leaders!). If it's from a male candidate, you are certain to see him with his shirtsleeves rolled up. Because, you know, he's going to work hard, get down to business, "roll up his sleeves!" for us.

While I find this amusing, candidates apparently do it because they know what works—and because they know that voters expect certain things from their politicians. Whether or not we care to admit it, while we may claim "anyone" can be president or a leader, really, we do have ideas on what a candidate should be experienced in, where they should come from, even what they should look like.

We aren't alone in this. I'm pretty sure that every civilization throughout history has had its own ideals of who their leaders should be as well. But as is almost always the case, these ideals we cling to are not the ones God seems to focus on.

Perhaps this is why I've always loved the idea of how God chose David. Sure, David was handsome and good with a slingshot, but he didn't seem to have a lot of typical "leadership experience."

According to today's verse, when God chose David, David was working in the sheep pens. Have you ever seen a sheep pen? I love animals—and sheep in particular—but yuck. There are flies. There are little mice. There is poop. Sheep pens stink. And yet, God took David from caring for sheep to become "the shepherd of his people Jacob."

I wonder if David ever saw this coming. I'd guess not. I'd guess David could've never imagined what God had in store for him as he went through his days of mucking out the pens, of tending the sheep. But that's how God is. Just as he doesn't look at political leaders the same way we do, nor does he look at *anyone's* potential the same way we do.

This is great news for us moms—especially during the seasons when we spend days on tasks that aren't much better than mucking out pens! Just as David was looked down upon for being a shepherd, so are moms often looked down upon for being, well, moms! But it's wonderful to imagine that even when we feel overwhelmed and yet "less than" for the amount of time we spend doing the "lowly" tasks of changing diapers, picking up toys, giving baths, preparing food, and scrubbing bathrooms, God is preparing us and has things in store for us that we can hardly imagine.

No matter where we are now, no matter what lowly tasks our days are filled with, God is preparing each of us for futures beyond what we might be able to imagine today. Our futures (and our present) are full of promise, full of wonder, full of amazement. And God is preparing us right now for those futures he has in store for us.

Response

God, prepare me for a future I cannot see. Give me the experiences and the courage I'll need to step into whatever plans you have laid out for me in these next stages of life. And on days when I feel lost in the humdrum ordinary of my life, remind me that all this honors you.

What does God say? See Jeremiah 29:11.

You Are Called to a Privileged Position

Psalm 25:14

The LORD confides in those who fear him;
he makes his covenant known to them.

I stayed silent as my friend raged on.

"I mean, God speaks to her and her alone? Is that what she's saying? Come on. Why would God speak to *her* and not to me?"

While trying to figure out care for their aging mother, my friend and her sister had gone to battle more than a few times. It only got worse when the sister shared something she believed God had told her.

Both sisters are Christians. Both seek to do the will of God. Both believe that God reveals his will in different ways. But when only one of them seemed to get a clear directive from God, it meant sibling war. At that point, the argument was no longer about what was best for their mother but about who was more special in God's eyes.

My friend wasn't angry that God apparently agreed with her sister. My friend was angry because God had chosen to *speak* to her sister. The sister had gotten a word from the Lord, while my friend got *nada*.

I stayed silent because I totally got what she was saying. I didn't want to fan the flames any more. But the truth is that though I have "heard" from God plenty of times in my life, I've also gone through seasons when I've heard nothing at all though I desperately needed a word or two. I've often wondered why some of us seem to hear so frequently from God while some of us only hear crickets chirping when we listen for him.

And during those times—when I long to hear from God but don't—I'm left feeling forgotten, not valued, unloved by God. This is how my friend felt too.

Though we may *feel* this way, the truth is quite different. God "speaks" to all of us. In different ways, I believe, according to who we are, to how well we are "listening," and to what we need. While my friend's sister got what she believed was a clear word from God, my friend's increasing lack of peace about the direction she had once believed was right for her mother turned out to be God speaking to her as well.

In times when I needed God's clear guidance, I may not have gotten the booming voice from heaven I longed for, but perhaps a serendipitous event, a line in a book, a passage of Scripture, the sight of a hawk, or the smell of my mother's fresh-baked cookies served as the word I needed.

Today's psalm says God "confides" in us and that he "makes his covenant known" to us. At least, to those of us who love him. This means that although God's messages may come in different forms and in different frequencies, we *all* share that privileged position of being confidants of God. He speaks to us. He walks with us. And if we pay attention, he makes his will known to us. Because he loves us and we are precious to him.

Response

God, I wish your will and your words to me were clearer than they sometimes are. I'd love an email—a text even!—from you telling me exactly what to do, exactly what I need to know. But help me notice your guidance and your words as you speak to me in other ways. Help me understand your will for my life however you choose to guide me.

What does God say? See Isaiah 42:16.

You Are Called to Take Bold Steps

Psalm 37:23–24

The LORD makes firm the steps
of the one who delights in him;
though he may stumble, he will not fall,
for the LORD upholds him with his hand.

My daughter amazed me. As soon as her skates were tightened and tied, Greta took to the ice like a champ. She eschewed the "ice walker" that could've helped her balance and instead grabbed my hand, wobbled a few times, and then straightened herself and pushed forward.

And there she went, ice-skating across the rink like she'd been doing this every day of her six years.

The first time Greta fell, she whimpered a bit. She dragged herself to the sides, pulled up, and pressed off again. As I skated behind her, I thought back to when she learned to walk. That had been different. She'd been a late walker. Then, just before she did learn to walk, she'd fractured her foot in a freak slide accident (yes, these do happen!). This set her back another month.

During that time when Greta had been so cautious about each step she took, I wondered what this would mean for her in life.

Would she always be so timid? Would she never learn to step boldly? Would she never take a risk?

While there had been plenty of other times when Greta proved just how unfounded my worries were about her being timid, watching her skate that day—and falling and getting back up—reminded me of how God really calls each of us to live. We were not made to hold tight to the edges of the rink, to eek and scootch along, ever fearful of falling. God intends for us to take bold strides or steps or leaps in whatever we are doing.

I'm not always so good at this. Often, I cling too much. I suppose it's my tendency to stay focused on the worrisome and fearful or on failing. I know I'm not alone here. Especially as moms who try to make life good for our families, we worry that our own bold steps might disrupt the family too much, that if we let go of the railings and push off we might fall and our families might suffer for our failing.

But I have to remind myself that this isn't the spirit of God. When David tells us that God "makes firm the steps of the one who delights in him" and reminds us that when we trip, "the LORD upholds [us] with his hand," David knows of what he speaks. David experienced both bold stepping and big stumbling. He knew both grand success and disastrous failure in his life. And yet, in each of those, David knew something else: God was with him.

Just as God is with us. Ready to help us in our steps as we go forward in life, ready to help us back up when we fall, and ready to walk with our families no matter where our bold steps might take us.

Response

God, each time I tumble, I'm tempted to stay put. To just lie on the floor of life and stop trying. But I know you call me to something else. I know you want me to get up and try again. Thank you for your promise to be with me as I stand back up and try again. Thank you for your patience and your mercy and your power-filling Spirit.

What does God say? See 2 Timothy 1:7.

You Are Called to Tap into God's Strength

Psalm 59:9–10

You are my strength, I watch for you;
  you, God, are my fortress,
  my God on whom I can rely.

My kids get excited to tell me about fitness tests in gym class. I smile through their stories and hug them about their successes, but on the inside I cringe at the very words *fitness test*.

My flashbacks to those days with the fitness tests that seem to thrill my kids today are nightmarish. Trying to climb the stupid rope. Trying to pull myself up on that stupid bar. Trying to maneuver those stupid pegs that fit into those holes. What was with that?!

Though I did well in nearly every area of school—and always loved school—PE was the one subject I failed at (well, not literally). I could not climb the rope, I could not pull myself up, and I could not do the peg-climb thing. I'm positive I still couldn't do any of them.

I am—in gym-class terms—not strong.

And yet, in real-world terms, I am quite strong. Always have been. I can endure quite a lot—both physically and emotionally. I am not a wimp, even though every PE class I ever took sure made me feel like one.

While I'm still no superhuman, when I've needed to be strong physically—whether to move furniture or haul children or reclaim lawn for the garden—strength has been there. When I've needed to be strong emotionally—walking beside my kids or husband through difficult circumstances—strength has been there.

My grade school PE teachers might be amazed, wondering where my strength all of a sudden came from, but I'm not. Maybe because I'm naturally weak, I'm aware that my strength comes from God. That he is the one to churn my muscles into action, to shore up my demeanor even when I feel like crumbling under the weight of worries.

God longs to fill us with his strength. He's done it for me. And he'll do it for you. So much of life—whether it's PE class or motherhood or trying to juggle family and work and everything else—stands to prove us weak. But God stands ready to prove us strong, in him.

We never need to be strong on our own, but instead we find our strength by falling back into *God's* power—or by "relying" on him, as today's psalm says. This is never more true than when we are attempting to do what God calls us to do. Perhaps I never could climb that rope because God didn't *call* me to do that. But if he had—or if he ever does—I know I will find my strength in him.

Response

God, I spend too much time focusing on my weaknesses and my faults. Help me instead to see the ways you step into my weak spots and I am made strong in you.

What does God say? See 2 Corinthians 12:7–10.

You Are Called to Serve a Great God

Psalm 86:10–12

For you are great and do marvelous deeds;
    you alone are God.
Teach me your way, Lord,
    that I may rely on your faithfulness;
give me an undivided heart,
    that I may fear your name.
I will praise you, Lord my God, with all my heart;
    I will glorify your name forever.

In my decade as a mom, I've spent a lot of time wondering who I was, who God made me to be, what he called me to do. Obviously, since the day my first child was born, I've known that part of me was made to be a mother, to raise the beautiful kids God gave me. I've known since the day we said our vows that I was called to be a wife to my husband. And I've been fairly certain (though it varies day by day) since age seven that God called me—created me!—to be a writer. And I know I'm called to be a good steward of all these gifts.

But even as I've known these things (and more) about who I was and who I was made to be, I've still wrestled—especially on the days when I felt like I was failing at every last calling. On the days when I was left too drained to be a very attentive wife or too frazzled to be a consistent mother or too overwhelmed to write a shopping list let alone a blog post, I felt like maybe God had made some serious mistakes when he made me the way he did.

And I think each of us always will—until we recognize what we've all been called to do. And that is simply to do our best at whatever we're doing, at whatever stage we are in life. We're to do it for God's glory. Because really, at the end of it all, more important than our callings as moms or wives or sisters or friends or whatever career or hobbies or volunteering we're engaged in, we are called to serve our mighty God. And we serve him by doing our *thing*—no matter what that thing is—for him.

While to some this may seem daunting—the idea of doing dishes or helping with homework or trying cases for God—in reality, it's so liberating. Because God doesn't expect perfection; he knows we will flub and fail in each of our callings. God wants our hearts, our minds, our bodies, and our souls focused on him as we live them out. When David asks God to teach him his "way" and to give him an "undivided heart," I sense this is what David was after: a way to serve his "great" and "marvelous" God in all that he did. Because it's when our hearts (and minds and souls and bodies) are undivided in purpose and attention, when we recognize that all we've been created to do is for God's glory, that we are able to serve God in all we do.

And when we do mess up—as we all will—he offers grace and forgiveness and second chances and all the things we've talked about in earlier devotions in this book. Simply because he loves us, he made us, we are his, and we are—above all else—called to serve our amazing God.

Response

God, thank you for accepting our best tries. And thank you for not minding when we mess up, but instead for being willing to step in and help sweep up the messes of our lives. Help me love you with everything I have—and in everything I do.

What does God say? See Deuteronomy 6:5.

Appendix A

About the Psalms

I've loved psalms since I was young. And even during spells when it was hard for me to read the Word of God because I didn't feel particularly "tight" with Jesus, psalms have beckoned me, compelled me with their beauty and rawness and truth. Psalms is easily my favorite book of the Bible.

And yet, as I sat down to write this appendix—to offer a few "need-to-knows" about the psalms—I realized how little I actually *knew* about them and how much I actually needed to know myself. So I went to my friend and teaching pastor, Gregg DeMey. Gregg loves psalms too; he steeps himself in them like I do, but he takes it much further. Gregg's read zillions of books about them, studied them in seminary, preached on them, and can read them (sort of) in Hebrew. Gregg is also a musician and has spent considerable time writing music for psalms. The psalm-inspired songs he's written are sung all over.

So over chai lattes and coffee at a local coffee shop, Gregg helped me hone in on a few key things that I—and everyone—should know about the psalms. While you could fill a library on things we *could* (and maybe should) learn about the psalms, I boiled it all down to three things.

#1: Psalms Were Sung

Though the words of the psalms have survived millennia, the music has not. We have no idea what these songs sounded like, but we do know that the words were to be set to music. We know this because many of the psalms contain a superscription to the "director of music." But we also know this because of the biblical poetic-prophecy tradition. According to Gregg, "Prophets in the Old Testament did their thing with musical accompaniment." Look no further than 2 Kings 3:15, when King Jehoshaphat calls for the prophet Elisha. Before he begins prophesying, Elisha calls for his harpist and "while the harpist was playing, the hand of the Lord came on Elisha."

It sounds over-the-top dramatic—even laughably so—but, according to Gregg, in the Bible, poetry, prophecy, and music go hand in hand. When I asked Gregg if it broke his musician heart *not* to be able to hear the psalm melodies, his response surprised me. While of course he'd love to know what they sounded like, Gregg wondered if God didn't have a big purpose behind keeping the melodies from us. After all, if we *had* the melodies, the psalms themselves might have died away as taste in music changed.

Beyond that, Gregg suggested that the music for the psalms could be looked at similarly to the infusion of the Holy Spirit, speaking to new generations of God-fearing folks. Meaning, by not having the melodies to accompany the psalms, the church has needed to insert the music throughout the ages, thus keeping the words and meaning fresh and "relevant" to each new generation.

Gregg also pointed out that David wrote Psalm 40 about God giving him a new song. Indeed, by not having music, the church gets the opportunity to sing new songs to old words and to express creativity. According to Gregg, when you pour the psalms into a new cultural form, they take on new meaning. Without music attached, the psalms are much freer, more easily adaptable to our lives.

#2: Psalms Are Poems—Sort Of

We all know the psalms are poems, but ancient Hebrew poetic conventions differ drastically from our idea of poetry. For instance, Hebrew poetry is nearly devoid of rhyme and meter and appears as prose on the written page.

So how do we know they are poetry? According to Gregg, the defining characteristic of Hebrew poetry is *parallelism*. In Hebrew poetry, we most often see two lines set together that illuminate one another. For instance, Psalm 120:4 says:

> He will punish you with a warrior's sharp arrows,
> with burning coals of the broom bush.

In this rather violent answer to what God will do to liars, we see two lines set together and illuminating one another: the burning coals shed some more light (and heat!) on the punishment.

We actually see this construction in other places in Scripture—even Jesus uses this poetic style. In Matthew 19:14, Jesus says, "Let the little children come to me, and do not hinder them, for the kingdom of heaven belongs to such as these."

You see that same parallelism when Jesus instructs the kids to come his way—and to not be hindered. It was an editorial choice not to print Jesus's words as poetry. This leads to the final point.

#3: Psalms Is a Book of Numbers

Although most poets probably wouldn't consider themselves "number people," if you know anything about or have spent any time studying poetry or lyrics, you know that numbers matter. Counting, to be specific, matters for all things rhythm and meter and rhyme.

The psalms are no different.

But beyond the numeric implications of each individual psalm, at some point one of the early "editors" of the psalms decided that numbers should play a role in the overall structure of the entire book.

Consider:

The book of Psalms is actually broken up into five books. Why five? We don't know. Some assume it's to correspond with the Pentateuch. But whatever the reason, these five books in Psalms have importance. "Knowing where a psalm comes in the big picture and in the smaller books makes a difference in how we understand it," said Gregg.

Someone at some time around 300 or 400 BC decided there should be 150 psalms. It's a good, round number. How do we know there weren't always 150? Because "clearly" some psalms have been broken up. Gregg said we know, for instance, that Psalm 42 and 43 were written as one psalm because they share the same chorus: "Why, my soul, are you downcast? Why so disturbed within me? Put your hope in God, for I will yet praise him, my Savior and my God."

Same goes with Psalm 111 and 112 because together they form an acrostic of the Hebrew alphabet.

Quick Facts about Psalms

- Each of the five books follows a theological assumption of "It always ends well with God." This assumption crescendos through the books until number 150—the ultimate praise psalm. But consider how Book III ends. The second-to-last psalm in that book is Psalm 88, the darkest lament in Psalms. Although Psalm 89 is slightly cheerier, scholars believe the final line of that psalm, "Praise be to the LORD forever! Amen and Amen" (separated by an extra line in most Bibles!), was tacked on by an editor in ancient times to support the assumption that it always ends well with God.

  Then, within those five books that make up Psalms, there are also other categories, like the Egyptian Hallel (Pss. 113–118), which were sung during Passover (Jesus would've sung these at the Last Supper) and the Psalms of Ascent (Pss. 120–134), which some believe were sung as Israelites ascended the hills into Jerusalem heading into the three annual Jewish feasts.

• Although the psalms are often attributed to David, he only wrote seventy-three or so of them. The rest were written by several authors. The authors we know of are David, Solomon, Asaph, Ethan, Heman, the sons of Korah, and maybe Moses. Not all the psalms have known authors.

• One-third of the psalms are laments—expressing disappointment or anger with God.

• Jesus quoted from Psalms more than from any other book of the Old Testament.

Appendix B

Write Your Own Psalm

Reading psalms leaves many of us grateful for words to express what we feel about God or our circumstances or life in general. But there's no reason we can't write our own words to describe those same things. So, if you've ever felt inclined to offer a few lines to God in praise and thanksgiving or in lament and frustration, now is your time!

In the following pages, you'll have a few options. You can write your own freestyle poem to God, choosing the Hebrew conventions and writing it devoid of meter and rhymes and with plenty of parallel lines. Or you can follow traditional poetry and pack your poem full of rhymes and rhythm. No reason you can't choose haiku, freestyle, a sonnet, a limerick, or whatever suits your mood.

Can't think of anything to write? Here are some prompts to get you thinking:

- How have you "seen" God in nature lately? What parts of creation have taken away your breath with their beauty? What have you heard, seen, smelled, felt, or tasted that made you marvel at God's goodness or creativity?
- What are you grateful for right now?

- What are you concerned about?
- What are you frustrated about?
- What are some prayers you are waiting for God to answer?
- What are some prayers God has answered in your life?
- What wonders are you hoping for God to work in your life?
- What unexpected blessings has God showered upon you?

Fill-in-the-Blank Psalm

If you have trouble writing your own psalm from scratch, why not "customize" an existing one? Try Psalm 13.

Psalm 13

How long, LORD? Will you

_____ (verb) me forever?
How long will you _____ (verb) your
_____ (noun) from me?
How long must I _____ (verb) with
my _____ (noun)
and day after day have _____
(noun) in my _____? (noun)
How long will my _____ (noun)
triumph over me?

Look on me and answer, LORD my God.
Give _____ (noun) to my _____,
(noun) or I will _____ (verb) in
_____, (noun)
and my enemy will say, "_____
_____," (taunt or brag)
and my foes will _____ (verb) when I
_____. (verb)

But I trust in your unfailing love;
   my heart rejoices in your salvation.
I will sing the LORD's praise,
   for he has been good to me.

Study Guide

This book is designed to be used either for personal spiritual growth or with a group. However you use the book, the time you invest in reading God's Word and reflecting on who you are in relationship to God is valuable.

If you are reading through individually, you can read the selections at your own pace and use these questions for reflections and journaling. Since there are fifty-two selections, you might decide to read one a day or one a week, but don't feel guilty if you miss a day or week. Just pick it up and start again!

While individual study is important, there is great value in exploring these topics with a group of women who are also seeking after God. You can learn together and encourage each other in your growth. Because the fifty-two devotions have been divided into ten sections, you can use this guide for a ten-session group study. Use it as a starting point and adapt it for your own needs. The questions will highlight a few devotions within each section. Feel free to emphasize different selections to meet the needs of your group. Keep your big-picture goal in mind as you spend time together in your group—to know God and yourself better by spending time in the psalms. See the special notes for group leaders.

Ground Rules for Group Study

Make your group a safe place for women to take risks and share their thoughts and questions as they explore their own identity and their understanding of God. Agree to confidentiality within the group so there is a safe atmosphere for sharing.

It may also be helpful to encourage women to stick to the Scriptures listed in the devotional for your discussion. Otherwise, women in your group with little knowledge of the Bible might be intimidated by participants who are citing lots of different verses. This focus will also help you keep discussions on track. Also encourage those who are more verbal to listen well and those who are quieter to feel free to share.

Format for Each Session

- Pray for the Holy Spirit to open your eyes to yourself, God, and others through the discussion.
- Start each session by reading aloud the theme psalm for that session.
- Open the conversation by asking participants which devotion in the section was most impactful for them and why.
- Use the specific questions provided.
- Apply the truth of each section by looking up the "What does God say?" verse or verses at the end and discussing how it applies to your personal journeys.
- Spend time praying for one another.

Session 1: You Are Wonderfully Made

You Are Made Just Right

- Share about ways you felt "just right" and ways that you felt "not right" as a child or adolescent.
- Do you carry some of your "not right" feelings into adulthood? Describe how this affects you now.
- How can Psalm 139 reshape your thinking about yourself?

You Are Given Unique Desires

- What are some of the unique desires God has placed on your heart?
- What would it look like for you to take a risk and move in the direction of the desires of your heart?

Session 2: You Are Held by God

You Are Sustained

- Caryn talks about the exhaustion of motherhood. Share about areas where you need physical or emotional strength for each day.

- What evidence do you see of God sustaining you? If this is hard for you to see, may others in the group encourage you by sharing some of God's basic daily sustenance?

You Are Heard

- Share some ways you feel silenced or invisible as a mom.

- Have you had experiences of sharing your voice and being heard? Share how that felt.

- How does the truth of God hearing you and caring for you increase your confidence?

Session 3: You Are Part of God's Story

You Are a Storyteller

- Think about your own life. Are there certain turning points or key story elements where you can see God's action in your life? Take some time to share a key life story with others in your group.

- Is there a part of your story that you don't like telling? (Group Leader: If the group is becoming a safe place, encourage these stories as well. Otherwise, encourage women to take personal time this week to acknowledge the hard parts of their stories. You may want to have access to counseling referrals if they are needed from this exercise.)

You Are a Conduit of Faithfulness

- Share places on your family tree where you can see God's faithfulness. If this is a hard exercise for you, think about how you are building your family now. Where can you see God's faithfulness in your family today?

- Dream about what your children will say about your family when they grow up. What sort of legacy do you want them to talk about? What are some small steps you can take to become this kind of family now?

Session 4: You Are a Work in Progress

You Are Refined by Motherhood

- Share about ways you have changed since becoming a mom.
- Caryn uses a remodeling analogy. What areas of your life have been "torn out" for you as a person?
- Have some parts of who you are been rebuilt through being a mom? Share about those areas.

You Are Affected by Choices

- What is the difference between consequences and forgiveness?
- Do you feel stuck in some bad choices you have made in the past? How can you experience redemption in those areas?
- As a mom, how do you respond to poor choices your children make?

Session 5: You Are Made in God's Image

You Are Creative

- Do you think of yourself as the "creative type"? Why or why not?
- What does it mean to you to be made in God's image, as a person who has the ability to be creative?
- Are there areas of creativity that you would like to explore and develop?

You Are Complex

- (Group Leader: Caryn refers to human resources interview questions on page 77. Use these questions in your group.)
- What descriptors can you use about yourself that go beyond your "mom" identity? "I am a mom and a _____."
- Is there an area of gifting or passion that you want to explore? What is holding you back from risking in this area?

Session 6: You Are Made for Many Things

You Are Made to Be Near God

- Describe a time when you have felt cozy and safe as a family.
- Caryn talks about how God wants his family (us) near to him too. What picture do you get when you imagine being close to God?
- What might be preventing you from drawing close to God?

You Are Made to Make Life Count

- Caryn describes her feelings of boredom during part of her season of being a mom at home. Do you share some of her feelings? Why or why not?
- Make a list of all the ways that what you do as a mom matters for your family, in both the long and short term.
- (Group Leader: If this exercise is hard for some, encourage each other in your group and add to each other's lists so that together you can see how much your lives do matter.)

Session 7: You Are Given Fresh Starts

You Are Healed from Wounds

- Are there areas of brokenheartedness that you have experienced or are experiencing?

- (Group Leader: If some are still in the midst of brokenheartedness, take some time in your group to pray together. Resist the urge to offer advice or want to "fix" another's heart. Just having a friend who will sit with us in brokenness is important.)

You Are Given a Second Chance

- Think about a past experience of a fresh start, such as a move or a new school year. Describe your feelings about this fresh and new time.

- Are there areas of mistakes or guilt that you feel stuck in? How can you make a conscious choice to move past guilt and know God's forgiveness?

- (Group Leader: Spend time encouraging each other regarding God's healing and forgiveness.)

Session 8: You Are Worthy

You Are Worthy of Maintaining Boundaries
- Caryn talks about the lack of defined time and space causing stress. On a scale of 1–10, how good are you at defining boundaries in your life? Discuss why you answered the way you did and describe your boundaries or areas that lack boundaries.
- How do you feel about setting boundaries in difficult areas?
- In what one area can you establish a boundary this week to value your worth in that area?

You Are Worthy of Being Still
- Have you experienced any "being still" time in the past week?
- What prevents you from finding space for your soul to be still?
- What is a practical way you can build time for stillness into your rhythm of life?

Session 9: You Are Loved by God

You Are Chosen

- Share a time of rejection or not being chosen from your childhood. What emotions and feelings does that experience bring up?

- Remember an experience of being chosen—in a relationship, in a job—and share how that experience made you feel.

- How does the truth of being chosen by God change your perspective on your daily life?

You Are Provided For

- When you think of "daily bread," what are the daily aspects of life that you are laying before God?

- How does your perspective of God change when you realize he cares about the "dailies" in your life?

- Share ways you have seen God's provision in the past. Consider keeping a journal of these experiences to build trust in God for the future.

Session 10: You Are Called and Equipped

You Are Mighty
- What animal would you pick to describe yourself and why?
- In what ways have you seen your protective love grow since having children?
- Share some areas where you feel less than mighty. Pray for each other in these areas.

You Are Called to Take Bold Steps
- Share about a time when you were learning a new skill. How did it feel? How did you grow in confidence?
- Is there currently an area where you are feeling called by God to step forward boldly? How does this psalm help you to be bold?
- (Group Leader: Take time to affirm and encourage each other in the ways God is causing growth and celebrate together.)

List of Devotions

Scripture Index

187

Caryn Rivadeneira, a writer and speaker, serves on the worship staff at Elmhurst Christian Reformed Church. She is the author of two books and former editor for several magazines. Caryn lives with her family just outside Chicago.

Meet Caryn at
carynrivadeneira.com

Read her blog, sign up for
her newsletter and more

Connect on

 caryn.rivadeneira

 @CarynRivadeneir

HOW CAN YOU LOOK TO THE FUTURE WHEN THE PAST SIMPLY WILL NOT LET YOU GO?

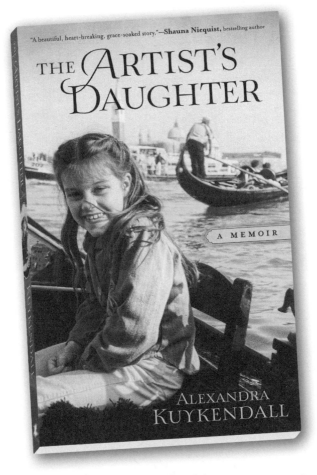

The Artist's Daughter will take you on a journey of discovery to answer three life-defining questions: Am I lovable? Am I loved? Am I loving? In Alexandra's story, written in short vignettes full of both wonder and heartaches, you will discover your own path to understanding the shape your life has taken—and a deeper sense of God's intimate guiding presence within it.

 Revell

a division of Baker Publishing Group
www.RevellBooks.com